Common Misconceptions of Economic Policy

Debunking Politically-charged and Emotionally-charged Assertions

By Jerry Wyant

With images by Cheryl Creech

Data graphs by Scott Haynie

Table of Contents

Introduction

Most people would probably admit that they know little about economics, and that they have little interest in undertaking an effort to learn more about the subject. This is understandable. Economics is a subject which has its own confusing terminology, lots of boring numbers (math and statistics, ugh!), theories, graphs, and especially disagreements among "experts".

Most people would not claim to be experts, but this does not stop them from publicizing their support for specific policies while demonizing any attempt to argue for alternative policies. Invariably, their positions on economic policies are based almost entirely on the emotionally-charged arguments espoused by politically-motivated advocates. They become pawns in a political game, accepting and spreading talking points from advocates who are not interested in telling the whole truth. Also invariably, they resist all opportunities to think through the issues thoroughly and without bias. They have their minds made up, and they are not at all interested in any contradictory facts or logic.

Many other people DO claim to base their opinions on a superior knowledge of economics, yet they still accept and spread misinformation. These are people who may have taken at least one economics course in school. Some of them might even be economics professors. They accept specific conclusions from economics models and theories, without understanding that in doing so they are ignoring relevant assumptions as well as fundamental economics concepts which supersede all assumption-based theories.

These are people who will tell you that their political viewpoint is the correct one because "anybody who knows basic economics knows this is true". Their arguments often boil down to something along the lines of "because it says so in Econ 101".

The "because it says so in Econ 101" argument is NOT a valid, logical argument. Yet even some economics professors and well-known economists use it frequently. A closer look at the issues for which this argument is used will often reveal that those making the case are leaving some important assumptions out of their arguments.

One case in point is the common "raising the minimum wage only hurts the people it is designed to help, and if you knew basic economics you would know that too" argument. I take on that argument in Section 9 of this book.

I am not a political junkie. I'm not interested in taking political talking points at face value. I'm not interested in simply repeating the talking points I hear. I'm not interested in mindlessly agreeing or disagreeing with somebody over politics, based on political labels.

I do like economics, though. I do believe in cutting through the partisan rhetoric and simplistic talking points in order to get to basic truths. I do believe in ignoring illogical arguments from partisan sources in order to get to basic truths.

Whenever I hear the same illogical talking points being repeated ad nauseam; whenever I see the same misinformation being spread on social media and elsewhere; and whenever I find people being misled by untruths, half-truths, and out-of-context facts designed to mislead people into supporting a political position which is otherwise not worthy of support – then I make an attempt to write about the specific issues involved from a rational and factual point of view.

This book is a selection of individual essays that I have recently published on key topics related to economic policy. Every essay in this book has been written for the purpose of debunking common misconceptions about how the economy works and the effects of economic policies.

The final section of the book provides examples of common illogical political statements, followed by a list of logical fallacies. Each of the other essays is dedicated to debunking a specific commonly-held misconception relating to economic policy or the way the economy works.

I do my best to write about economics in language that is easy to understand for everyday citizens - those who are unfamiliar with or uncomfortable with the language of economics. The essays in this book have been written with such a reading audience in mind. My hope is that if you have reading comprehension skills, you can understand what I am trying to say, even if you tend to shy away from the subject of economics.

The only exception is the previously-mentioned essay about the minimum wage. For that one, I use the same types of economic theory, graphs, and language that is used in the arguments that my essay is designed to debunk.

For the remainder of the book, I use – as much as possible and to the best of my ability – everyday language to point out commonly-held misconceptions of several topics relating to economic policy and the economy. In this book, you will find essays on common misconceptions in topics such as taxes; unemployment; inflation; income inequality; deficits and debt; Social Security; welfare; and the roles that market forces, corporations, and the government play in the economy.

I am not using this book as a platform to use political labels and political talking points in order to make political statements based on a predetermined political position. My agenda is to use truth and logic in order to debunk such statements. People will find that the conclusions I reach tend to fall towards the progressive – rather than the conservative – end of what the political spectrum has become in modern times. I already know that many people who blindly follow conservative talking points will see my conclusions and denounce what I have to say, based solely on a liberal label that they attach to me, with no regard for the actual points I make. This happens all the time. They can't – or at least they choose not to – logically rebut the actual points being made. Instead, they commit several logical fallacies (Section 12) through a personal attack. But they are not alone. On those occasions when my conclusions don't coincide with commonly-held liberal positions, I get the same treatment from those who blindly follow liberal talking points.

I have found that the truth does not lie on the side of anybody's talking points. I have also found that the truth cannot be found by making an attempt to balance opposing talking points. The truth can only be found through an unbiased search for the truth. That truth is rarely found straight down the center. I have concluded that it is dishonest as well as illogical to tailor an argument so that it agrees with the left, the right, or the center. The truth is what it is, regardless of labels. I do not manipulate the truth so that it agrees with a political position. I adjust my political position so that it agrees with whatever truths I find.

***

The essays in this book were originally published in The Blue Route Blog and in my personal blog at www.economicsonlinetutor.com/blog.

This book is a follow-up to *Sanity and Public Policy: Separating Truth from Truisms*, by Jerry Wyant.

~ Jerry Wyant, author of *Common Misconceptions of Economic Policy*

Section 1: Fundamentals of the Economy

Social Structure, Government, and Economics

(Originally published August 4, 2014 for The Blue Route Blog)

Economics as a field of study is generally taught as stemming from questions of resource allocation: the what, how, and who questions of production and distribution. What they do not generally teach is the process by which this relates to the very basics of social structure and the formation of government. This short list provides some of the important points in the process.

Follow along with these points in order, as if this were a step by step process, in order to grasp the logic.

1. Human greed cannot be eliminated. It cannot be wished away and it cannot be legislated away.

2. As long as greed exists, people will exist who will never be satisfied with what they have. Somebody will always want more possessions and more power, no matter how much they already have.

3. Without social control, the incentive for the greedy to acquire power will be strong enough for the greedy to become the powerful.

4. In the natural state, without social control, wealth always goes to the already-powerful.

5. The most powerful individuals, motivated by greed, will control everything unless social controls are created.

6. The more that powerful individuals control, the less there is for everybody else.

7. Desperation becomes a motive for theft. Theft and greed become motivations for many types of crimes, including violent crimes.

Indeed, most crimes result from greed, desperation, or both. Between greed and desperation, all social structures break down.

8. This situation means that the only connection to wealth is power. Power creates wealth relative to the powerless and this wealth can be used to create more power. Power and wealth feed on each other, creating a small wealthy class. Wisdom, generosity, a sense of humanity, safety, freedom, and the like play no role in determining who is powerful and rich.

9. With wealth and power increasingly going to whoever already has both, the incentive for the powerless to contribute to the economy by creating something that will increase the standard of living is nonexistent.

10. The end result is massive poverty, hunger, and an inevitable higher death rate.

11. Social unrest and revolution are also inevitable results. This can eliminate the powerful in the short run, but it cannot eliminate greed. A new cycle of power and greed feeding off of each other will begin.

12. Social control is the only way to prevent this outcome. Laws are established. This is called government.

13. This kind of government is not the same thing as the rich and powerful passing laws to control everybody else and to protect what they already have taken. "Government" by the rich and powerful is not really government at all. Instead, it is only a step in the power-and-wealth-feeding-off-of-each-other cycle. The kind of government that results in social control is government "for the people".

14. Since a lack of government means that all of the wealth and power go to those who already have wealth and power, and since government is formed for the people in order to prevent the inevitable undesirable outcomes that this cycle of wealth and

power creates, then what kind of outcome in terms of the distribution of wealth and power should the government for the people aim for? What methods should the government use to bring about a more desired outcome? What methods and outcomes would create a more desirable society? If wealth naturally moves upward towards the rich and powerful, eventually resulting in a breakdown in society and massive poverty, how much of this natural upward redistribution can be said to create a desirable outcome, or should this redistribution not occur at all? How much should contributions of wealth be rewarded, and how much should contributions of labor be rewarded? If equal outcome is the only goal, regardless of contribution, does this create a low level of living standard, due to a decrease in incentives? If contributions of wealth are rewarded more than contributions of labor, how much poverty, sickness, and death associated with poverty is acceptable to society as an outcome of rewarding wealth with more wealth? If neither the extreme of all wealth being centralized in few hands nor the extreme of equal outcome regardless of contribution are desirable, what kind of balance between the two extremes would be desirable? What method of reaching such a balance is acceptable? If fairness is a major concern, then whose idea of fairness should prevail?

15. Mankind has created different points of view in terms of answers to these questions. These viewpoints, the answers to these questions, go directly to the heart of all political and economic systems.

Follow the Money

(Originally published August 4, 2014 for The Blue Route Blog)

The money trail will always tell us what we value as a society.

Look to see where the money goes. Take a look at who gets it and what it is used for. That will tell you exactly what we value in our society.

This is true regardless of the type of political system. It is true regardless of the type of economic system. It is true for all economic policies. It is true for free markets.

The only exceptions are those who are economic slaves. These are people who have absolutely no recourse in having their values reflected in the type of society that they are forced to live in. They have no economic power and they have no political power. They cannot vote (or they live in a society in which their votes don't really count), they cannot hold a political office from which they can make a difference, and they cannot join forces in order to gain political or economic power. They have no say in the type of society that they live in, and they have no power to change this situation. These people are invisible when it comes to society's values. The money trail reflects the cumulative values of everybody else.

What you choose to do with your own money reflects your values. What you buy with this money reflects your values. Where the money goes after you spend it is also part of the money trail, and it will be a reflection of your values. Your values create this money trail and the money trail will lead to specific results in society. If you save or invest money, then what happens to that money in the hands of others will also be part of the money trail that you have created through your values. This money trail leads to specific results for you and for society. Only real results matter; theoretical outcomes do not.

You even make choices which determine where you get your money, and how much you get. This too reflects your values. How these choices affect other people in society reflect your values. Sometimes, people make money in ways that benefit others, and sometimes people make money in ways that exploit others – these are results of values. There is a money trail that will determine these results.

Government policies that you choose to support or oppose also involve real results that affect real people and society in general. Theories and philosophy will not determine what these results are, but the money trail will. Each policy option will alter the real outcome by altering the money trail. How policies affect real people, and how potential policies would affect real people, as determined by how the policies alter the money trail, reflect the values of those who support these policies.

If you know that specific outcomes will result from your choices, and you are okay with those outcomes, then those outcomes become something that you value.

You don't have to tell me what you value, what I value, or what we value as a nation. The money trail will tell me that. The only thing that matters is the end result. Don't tell me that you value one economic or political philosophy over another, or which economic theories you subscribe to, or why. Don't tell me that you value human life; or that you support the notion that "all men are created equal"; or that you have Christian values; or anything else using similar language about values. The actual results from the policies you support in the real world for real people will tell me what you value. The results matter and nothing else does. If you support policies which cause pain and suffering, starvation, and even death, then those are real results that reflect your values. Theories and philosophy are irrelevant if the real-world results tell a different story.

If you see economic injustice, do you ignore it, because it reflects your own values? Do you complain about it, but still support the policies that brought about the injustice? Do you excuse it, because it is a natural result of a system that you support?

Or would you support making changes that address the injustice? Would you be willing to spend more of your money to decrease injustice, or would you continue to spend your money in ways that contribute to injustice?

The way that your choices create real results for real people reflects your values. Follow the money, and you will be able to see these results.

What you say you value and what you claim are your political and economic philosophies, or even your religious beliefs for that matter, mean very little if your choices create a money trail that says something else entirely.

Section 2: The Role of Market Forces in the Economy

Unrestricted Free Markets

(Originally published January 4, 2015 for The Blue Route Blog)

"Unrestricted free markets" is a term which makes no economic sense.

An economic policy is a law, regulation, practice, or strategy which affects an economy. Within any economy, the existing set of economic policies constitutes an economic system. Each economic system is unique, because each economy has its own set of policies. People like to use labels to define these systems, so we always hear about capitalist policies and socialist policies, with individual policies as well as entire economic systems critiqued according to how the observer perceives them in terms of capitalism and socialism.

In any economic system, market forces are going to be present. No government has ever been successful in creating an economy void of market forces. No government has ever successfully eliminated market forces from an existing economy. Economic facts of life include the presence of market forces. At the same time, no economic system can exist without a framework provided by a governmental power. If there is no framework, then there is no civilization, and any economy will collapse very quickly. Market forces require a governmental framework. Market forces require the presence of an infrastructure. Market forces require the existence of economic policies, whether the policies are considered to be activist or not. Economic results depend on the costs and benefits of the specific policies in place. Costs and benefits involve the effects of policies on the overall economy as well as specific effects on individuals and groups of individuals in the economy.

Since economic results depend on the policies in place, the distribution of income depends on the policies in place. A specific distribution of income in the past was influenced by the policies in place at that point in time. A specific distribution of income today is influenced by the policies in place today. Since the economy requires economic policies to be in place, there has never been a time in the past which anybody can point to and accurately state that "the income went to those who earned it". Policy changes have taken that away. This includes the effects on the economy of tax rates, tax breaks, regulations, and any other policy affecting the economy. Policy changes will affect the distribution of income, but this doesn't automatically mean that the old way was better for the economy – or for society in general – than the new way.

In terms of the rhetoric labelling every policy or system as being either capitalist or socialist, the rhetoric is far from the reality. It is just that – rhetoric. There have been some governments, notably communist regimes, which have relegated market forces to the underground economy and officially denied the existence of market forces. But market forces were always at work within these economic systems, even if they were not allowed to work efficiently. There are economies with nationalized industries for various reasons – reasons such as the importance of the industry to the national interest, as a type of trade restriction, or even for national security. I should note that the definition of socialism is government ownership of the means of production. Nationalized industries are socialist subsets of national economies. The United States does not have nationalized industries. When I hear people using rhetoric such as "the federal government doesn't produce anything", my answer is: Of course they don't produce anything. That's not their job. They provide the infrastructure and the economic framework which allows the private sector to produce goods and services in the economy.

According to this definition of socialism – that the government owns the means of production – there is nothing socialist about the economic system in the United States. The private sector owns the means of production. Still, people like to use labels, so they redefine socialism to include any policies which increase the government's regulation of the economy; policies which put more people on the government's payroll; policies which create a safety net for individuals; policies which create automatic stabilizers to mitigate the consequences of recessions; some or all aspects of taxation; and the like. Using this wider definition of socialism, and noting that market forces are always at work in every economy, then the best we can do is state that every national economy in the world is to some degree a mixed economy (combination of capitalist and socialist). There are varying degrees of this mixture, and each economy is unique in the details.

I hear people advocating for "unrestricted free markets". I have no idea what they are talking about. This language is used in conjunction with "getting the government out of the way so that the market can work its magic". I don't think advocates know what that means. Put simply, there is no such thing as "unrestricted free markets". And the "magic" of free markets that some people expect if government "gets out of the way" cannot exist either.

There is nothing magical about how the economy works. The "invisible hand" which supposedly benefits society in some magical fashion is not something that occurs in the absence of a structured society. Government policies WILL affect economic outcomes. If the party on one side of an economic transaction is free to exploit the party on the other side of that transaction, then the "invisible hand" will not work to benefit society. It only makes sense, in terms of economic outcomes, when the "free" in "free markets" means that each side is equally free to accept or decline any potential transaction. This includes labor markets as well as product markets. If one side doesn't have all of the relevant information that the other side has, then there is nothing "free" about that market. If one side is more desperate to complete a transaction than the other side, there is nothing "free" about that

17

market. Only when the sides in each potential transaction have equal market power is the market truly "free".

Freedom to exploit means freedom for those with less market power to be exploited. The "invisible hand" works when each side is free, through equal market power, to pursue its own self-interest. The absence of government regulation does not create a situation of "free markets" – it creates freedom to exploit. Government policies which provide producers with more market power than consumers, or which provide consumers with more market power than producers, do not create free markets. Government policies which provide employers with more market power than employees, or which provide employees with more market power than employers, do not create free markets. History repeatedly bears this out.

Many people support "free markets" because of a perceived connection between free markets and personal freedom. Personal freedom does not come to individuals if their lack of market power allows them to be exploited. Personal freedom and free markets are not going to result from giving exploiters more power to exploit.

Markets can be "unrestricted." Markets can be "free." But markets cannot simultaneously be "unrestricted" and "free".

Personal freedom and free market forces come with the correct use of the government's economic structure, with the correct economic policies. Of course the economy can suffer from ill-conceived regulations. But the economy can also suffer from not having a regulation which would be good for the economy. There can be too much government. But there can also be too little government. The government could have the wrong set of economic policies in place, but that doesn't automatically equate to having too many government policies. Taxes are necessary, but the tax code can overly burden certain groups of taxpayers. Taxes can be too high;

government spending can be too high. It depends on the results of policies, taking into consideration all costs and all benefits.

A blanket statement saying that taxes and government spending need to be cut, without properly addressing all of the costs and benefits, is not an advocacy for a better society. Rhetoric that cherry-picks certain costs and ignores all of the benefits of a type of policy, in order to make the case that less is more, is neither logical nor honest. An honest and thorough assessment of costs and benefits of specific policies can lead to better policy. But blanket rhetorical statements cannot.

"Unrestricted free markets" is a misnomer. The term makes no economic sense.

Market Forces and the Real World

(Originally published January 25, 2015 for The Blue Route Blog)

If you believe in an economy which relies on market forces, like I do, you might not have considered these important and basic truths…

Market forces are not natural forces which exist independently of everything else. In order for market forces to work their "magic", they must exist within a social framework. Without a government to provide a framework, market forces as we think of them would not exist.

Economic outcomes depend on the details of the government's framework. Every policy which affects the economy will alter the outcome and become part of the framework. This includes unintended consequences of seemingly non-economic policies. Since policies are constantly being altered on some level, the framework is fluid. The world itself is constantly changing. New technology and other changes in real-world conditions affect the results of specific policies.

For example, somebody might find a way to exploit new technology to gain an unfair economic advantage. Or perhaps somebody will figure out a loophole in current law and gain an unfair advantage; an advantage which runs counter to the intention of the law. When such changes occur in the world, economic outcomes of existing policies also change. When a new policy is implemented to correct for such undesirable outcomes, then the government's framework also changes.

There is no single set of policies from any time frame that we can rightly point to – and state unequivocally - that those policies are the best possible policies for all time. There is no such thing as an economic system that is a pure market economy. Every economic system is the sum of all policies which affect the economy. Every economic system is unique.

We can't point to "no government" as a desirable market system. A market system doesn't exist without government. We can't honestly state that "less government" is always better regardless of the current situation. The natural outcome of less government as a continuing policy is going to be no government; the result would be that no market economy could exist.

We also can't honestly state that "more government" is always a better solution.

What is important is to understand the outcomes of policies. Do specific policies create desirable or undesirable outcomes? Who gets to decide what a desirable outcome is? (Hint: "We the People") It takes simplistic thinking to frame every economic issue in terms of "too much" or "too little" government. The existence of government is a necessity. The size of the government alone is not a factor in determining the desirability of economic outcomes. Only the specific outcomes of specific policies matter. A policy may have desirable outcomes. A policy may have undesirable outcomes. A policy may have mixed outcomes, leaving its net benefit open to debate. What matters is whether the outcomes of the policy are desirable.

When I hear people express opposition to a policy because it is a "big government" policy, instead of demonstrating knowledge of the actual economic outcomes of the policy, I know that these people are using simple-minded thinking. When I hear people state that "less government is always better" or "government is always the problem", I know that these people are using simple-minded thinking. People who believe such claims are not aware of how things work in the real world.

When I hear people constantly argue against policies they don't agree with on the basis that such policies represent "socialism", I know that these people do not know what they are talking about. We do not have socialist (read: government ownership of the means of production) policies in the United States, and there are no serious proposals on the table for such policies. When I hear people claim that proposed policy changes, designed to correct for unintended or undesirable consequences, are "redistributions" that are somehow unfair – yet these same people avoid mentioning the earlier policy changes which created the undesirable consequences – I know that these people don't know what they are talking about. Unfortunately, there is no shortage of politicians and pundits who will repeat such nonsensical claims so often that honest yet gullible people actually believe them.

When I hear people boast that they only listen to people who tend to make such claims, and ignore all other sources, I know that these people do not value the truth. They don't care about real economic outcomes as much as they value partisanship.

Market outcomes do not occur by magic. There is logic to how the economy works, but not everyone is willing and able to learn the logic. You won't find the truth by relying solely on sources which will provide you with simplistic talking points. Those sources rely on your ignorance and gullibility.

A Market-Based Economy is a Pass-Through Economy

(Originally published April 21, 2015 for The Blue Route Blog)

Middle class economics and reversing the Citizens United ruling are both themes which promise to become major issues during the upcoming 2016 general election season. Here is an explanation for why these are important issues.

The economy is all about activity. We produce goods and services, and we buy goods and services. We invest, and we save. We hire workers, or we are the workers hired by others. We innovate, or we enjoy an increase in the standard of living because others have been innovators. As individuals, we participate in the economy in various ways.

You might not have thought about it in these terms, but in order to understand how the economy works, and why it doesn't always work to our satisfaction, you should be aware that the economy is a pass-through economy. Economic activities are all inter-related. In order to produce anything, you need to be motivated to do so. Your motivation comes from the expectations of profit. But you won't get profit unless you have customers willing and able to buy what you produce. If your customers don't have the means to pay for what you produce, then you have no reason to produce.

Labor markets, financial markets, foreign markets, and the government all play roles in this. Without going into detail on these various roles (because that would be going off-topic), my point is this:

Wealth and financial assets keep the economy growing, keep the economy producing, keep people employed, and increase the standard of living – but ONLY as long as wealth and financial assets continue to PASS THROUGH from one sector of the economy to another. When wealth and financial assets are taken out of the loop, they no longer benefit the economy. In order for wealth to benefit the economy, it has to keep circulating throughout the economy. That's what makes it a pass-through economy.

None of this is a secret. It's a design feature of a market-based economy. Have you heard of the "invisible hand" in economics? A pass-through economy is necessary for the invisible hand to work its magic. The government provides the infrastructure which is necessary for the economy to even exist. The government provides incentives, especially tax incentives, designed to promote economic activity. Businesses do not pay taxes based on the amount of total revenue. Instead, businesses are allowed to deduct all business expenses before taxes. This includes the amount paid for employee wages and benefits. Tax deductions provide an incentive for more money to continue to pass through the economy. Progressive income taxes on earnings net of business expenses decrease the cost of keeping wealth working through the economy RELATIVE TO the cost of taking wealth out of the economy. Capital gains receive favorable tax treatment.

Why does the government provide these incentives? Keep in mind that these are the fundamental ways in which the government "interferes" with the private sector in the economy. Incentives are designed to keep wealth passing through the economy. The health of the economy and the standard of living depend on it. If you make money, you can make even more money if you invest it back into the economy. There is actually no upper limit to how much you can make with these incentives; they allow individuals to get ahead through hard work and innovation, which provides an incentive for others to work hard and innovate. The good news for everybody is that all of this benefits the economy. There is nothing socialistic about any of this. The more money you put back into the economy, the more money you can make. The more money you make, the more you can put back into the economy. The better your investments perform, the more money you can make BECAUSE your investments are benefitting everybody in a pass-through economy.

Without the benefits of a pass-through economy, all arguments claiming that a market-based economy is superior to other economic systems fall apart.

That's how it is supposed to work. That is the basis of a market-based economy. Economic activity occurs in the private sector. The government provides infrastructure. Wealth is rewarded with more wealth when it is being used to benefit the economy. It is in the national interest for the government to provide incentives to make this happen. Rewarding people for allowing their wealth to pass-through within the economy is essential to a market-based economy.

BUT IT DOESN'T ALWAYS WORK THAT WAY. Laws are being written in order to provide incentives for NOT letting wealth pass through within the economy. Wealth is being removed from the economy, and the culprits are being rewarded for doing so.

Not all types of "investments" receiving preferential tax treatment are actually investments back into the economy.

Tax cuts for NOT investing actually INCREASE the cost of putting wealth to work in the economy RELATIVE TO the cost of taking wealth out of the economy.

Corporations are being rewarded with tax breaks for removing wealth from the country and from the domestic economy – and for taking jobs out of the country.

Labor laws are being weakened, decreasing the amount of money that flows through the working class and into the wider economy.

Wealth is being removed from the pass-through economy via corporate tax breaks handed out by all levels of government, instead of providing infrastructure improvements that are vital for the economy to operate smoothly.

Instead of using cash to invest in the pass-through economy, corporations are being rewarded for using that cash to finance political campaigns, for hiring lobbyists, and for a media campaign on their behalf – all for the purpose of receiving incentives to remove wealth from the pass-through economy.

As a result of misguided policies…

1. ALL wealth created through economic growth and productivity has been retained by the extreme upper class – this is not a theory or a political point of view; it has been an economic fact since the late 1970s.

2. Our infrastructure is crumbling.

3. The most vulnerable of us – the elderly, the young, the poor, and the sick – are being told that they will have to get by with less in order for corporations to receive more tax breaks.

4. The middle class is shrinking, fewer people are making a living wage, more people are making poverty wages, more people must rely on public assistance, and politicians are joining the media chorus in blaming the victims – "hey, the rich pay all the taxes and the poor are free-loading off of tax dollars from the rich, so let's cut government spending on programs which benefit the poor, and instead let's cut taxes for the rich who are paying all of the taxes" and "hey, those who complain about this are lazy people who are engaging in class warfare" – thereby advocating for more of the same types of policies which created the problem in the first place.

Too many people don't understand the relationships among incentives, policy, infrastructure, income, tax rates, and tax dollars. This is unfortunate, because it means that not only do people support policies which are against their own self-interest, they also support policies which undermine the entire economy. The political and media chorus only confirms their misconceptions.

Here is a reality based on mathematical truth: Top marginal corporate and individual income tax rates are extremely low by historical standards – much lower than the rates which were in effect when the middle class was growing and the United States reached economic superstar status – despite widespread political rhetoric about stifling tax rates on the rich. Once you grasp that fact, consider this mathematical fact: The amount of tax dollars paid is equal to the effective tax rate times the amount of taxable income. When effective tax rates become LESS progressive, which they have, and yet a larger percentage of tax dollars is being paid by those at the high-end of the income scale, it can only mean one thing: a larger share of the income has stayed at the top. High tax rates on those at the top didn't cause this to happen, and lowering high-end tax rates won't fix it. This problem was created because less wealth has been passing through the economy. It was created by policies which increase the incentive to take wealth out of the economy. Lowering corporate and high-end tax rates will provide more of an incentive to take wealth out of the economy. It will mean more of the same policies which created the problem.

Math, basic economic principles, rational thinking, and the historical record all point to this reality. Unfortunately, too many people ignore all of that in favor of political rhetoric which doesn't agree with reality. This situation is not sustainable, but as long as so many people are falling for the rhetoric instead of the reality, it might have to get much worse before it gets better. The rhetoric is allowing the few to profit at the expense of the many until reality sets in.

A sustainable and smooth-running market-based economy requires rewards for allowing wealth to pass through the wide economy. Policies which hand out rewards for taking wealth out of the pass-through process can only undermine the economy. Either we wait until the situation gets so bad that it wakes people up to the reality, or we find a way to get more of them to see the reality today. A highly publicized general election campaign focused on middle class economics and reasons for reversing the Citizens United ruling is a small step towards educating the population to economic realities.

Section 3: Causes and Consequences of Rising Economic Inequality

Job Creators, Taxes, and Inequality

(Originally published August 5, 2014 for The Blue Route Blog)

"Corporations are job creators."

"We would have more jobs if taxes on the rich were lower."

"Taxing the rich takes money away from those who earn it."

"Corporations would create more jobs if the government would let them keep more of their money."

"The reason why the economy is hurting is because of oppressive taxes on the rich and on corporations."

"Progressive taxes and welfare are socialist wealth redistributions that destroy the economy."

"If you raise taxes on job creators, it will destroy the economy".

We hear such statements ad nauseam. Surely they must be true if everybody is saying so, right? Even raising revenue for the government by closing tax loopholes for the wealthiest is considered heresy. If we close these loopholes, it amounts to "raising taxes on job creators".

What are the merits of such claims? Would raising taxes on the rich be a job-killer, because that is what happens when you tax "job creators"?

The first question to ask is this: are rich corporations and individuals really job-creators? For the sake of argument, let's just assume for now that they are. So, will raising taxes on these job creators really kill jobs?

Let's think through the process of how this all works. Instead of relying on some vague theory or political rhetoric, think through the actual process. First of all, income taxes, whatever the rates, only apply to pretax gains. The original investment is not taxed, only the gains. For any given income tax rate, people can use their BEFORE-TAX income on something that can be written off on their tax return, thus reducing their taxes, or they can use this income on something that WON'T reduce their taxes. In that case, they will be paying taxes at the marginal rate on that income. If they hire workers, and therefore "create jobs", then the salaries and benefits that they pay out to workers become business expenses. They won't pay taxes on this money because it is deducted from revenue before computing taxable income. If they decide not to hire workers, and keep the money as profits, then they WILL have to pay taxes on this money. Unless they find somewhere else to invest the money, an investment in something that does NOT create jobs, they will have to pay taxes on this money. But if they hire workers with the money, then they won't have to pay taxes on it. That is how the tax code works. Hire workers, pay fewer taxes. Don't hire workers, and either pay more taxes or invest in something that doesn't create jobs.

To repeat: for any given tax rate, hire workers and pay fewer taxes. Don't hire workers, and either pay more taxes or invest in something that doesn't create jobs. That is what happens for any given tax rate. What happens when the tax rate changes?

If you increase the tax rates on these job creators, then the tax that they pay on everything EXCEPT jobs will go up. They still won't have to pay taxes on the money that they spend for employee compensation. A tax increase will give them an incentive to invest in the business, because it is the cost of NOT investing that goes up. The cost of investing does not increase. An increase in the income tax rate won't give them an incentive NOT to invest in job creation. This will not be an incentive for killing jobs; it will be an incentive for creating jobs. Job creation takes money out of the column that is taxable and puts it in the column that is not taxable. This is simple mathematics; not political rhetoric, but mathematics.

If you decrease the tax rates on these job creators, then there will be no added incentive to create jobs. The amount of income taxes paid on employee salaries and benefits for these job creators is zero either way. What a tax rate decrease does is decrease the taxes that they have to pay on the money that they aren't using to create jobs anyway. The cost of paying for jobs does not go up, but the cost of NOT creating jobs goes down. It is an incentive for them to keep more profits that are taxable. It is in no way an incentive for them to spend the money on job creation; again, mathematics and not rhetoric.

Please re-read from the beginning if you don't understand this concept so far. This is a concept that is important to our economy today. It explains to a large degree how we have been spending so much time struggling through a "jobless recovery" even as large corporations are reporting record profits and record cash levels. These corporations already have more cash than they are investing back into their businesses. Interest rates for them to finance job creation through borrowing are at historical lows, near zero. Yet they aren't investing this money on jobs. The wealthiest individuals have recovered from the recession while the incomes of everybody else have fallen, increasing the already-wide wealth gap. With this amount of cash and job-creating ability already, why do we have so many unemployed people? The political rhetoric is that these job creators just need one more benefit from us, on top of their record cash reserves, in the form of lower taxes, in order for them to have an incentive to create jobs. Or that the millions of unemployed Americans are all lazy anyway. Or that somehow, these workers aren't qualified to take back the jobs that they were laid off from.

That is the political rhetoric. The reality is something different entirely. The reality is that: (1) raising taxes on the rich doesn't kill jobs, and lowering taxes on the rich doesn't create jobs, as explained above; and (2) the rich are not the real job creators, as explained below.

For the above explanation about taxes, I left in the assumption that the rich are the ones that create jobs in order to focus on the effects of tax rates for the richest Americans. But the truth is that consumers are the ones that create jobs. Tax rates for the rich have nothing to do with it. If a business of any size sees a way to increase before-tax profits, it would be to their advantage to do so. They want to keep their tax bills at a minimum, of course, but raising before-tax profits will also raise after-tax profits. Very little money for rich individuals and for corporations will be caught up in the margin where the additional before-tax profits will be lower than the additional taxes. If any business decision-makers worry about the taxes more than the actual effects on the bottom line, then they aren't making wise decisions. Increasing before-tax profits for all practical purposes is the same thing as increasing after-tax profits.

If businesses or potential businesses see a demand for their products and/or services that will generate a profit, they will do what they can to get that profit. If it means hiring more workers in order to meet that demand, and the cost of additional workers is lower than the addition to potential profits, then they will hire more workers. The income tax rate on the business has nothing to do with it. What is needed to make it all happen is consumer demand. The people who will do the buying in the economy are the ones who need the buying power to make it all happen. It is a consumer-driven economy. More income for the middle class, for the working poor and even for the non-workers will create demand. Consumer income and consumer confidence in the economy create jobs.

I mentioned consumer confidence. What about business confidence? Business confidence starts with consumer demand. If the masses in the population aren't buying, then there won't be any business confidence. Businesses prefer stable government policies for sure, but most business owners won't tell you that stable higher income tax rates will create just as much business confidence, in terms of creating jobs, as stable lower income tax rates. But that is the truth. Eliminating loopholes will create more stability than anything, because it levels the playing field. Businesses will quit scrambling around, paying expensive tax lawyers and accountants to look for loopholes if the loopholes no longer exist.

The rich benefit financially, and directly, from the infrastructure more than the poor do. The rich benefit from the spending patterns of the poor, through investments. The more money the poor have to spend, the more income the rich make off of domestic investments. Businesses (and investments) are successful only if the economy produces enough demand.

So, you don't want to raise taxes on "job creators"? Then quit demanding that the poor pay more taxes. Quit backing policies that have been destroying the middle class for the past 30 years. Prior to 1981, incomes for all classes rose together as the economy grew. The upper classes got more than the lower classes, but all gained at equivalent rates. Since then, the top 10% have received more than the rest. Even the gains of the top 10% have paled in comparisons to the gains of the top 1%. Those are economic facts that are readily available to anybody who cares to fact-check any of this. All of this is the result of changes in economic policies in Washington. These policies have created a situation in which income that would have been distributed throughout all income levels, based on policies that were in effect from the 1950s all the way through 1980, is now all going directly to the top. And this income is staying at the top. It is not trickling down. Wealth has been redistributed; but not from rich to poor like the political rhetoric says. Wealth never gets redistributed from rich to poor in the United States today. It always gets redistributed from poor and middle class to rich. The wealthiest have always received the most income, as a group. But the redistribution has occurred because of policy changes that have allowed those at the very top to keep all of the income gains, including the income that used to go to the middle-class. The American Dream of upward mobility is available to fewer and fewer people.

Here is a related hot issue that is driven by rhetoric: why raise taxes on the rich when they already pay most of the taxes? Well, they pay most of the income taxes, but not most of the other taxes. The other taxes are mostly regressive. The income tax used to be very progressive to balance this out. History shows that rhetoric stating that our current problems are caused by "oppressive" income taxes on rich individuals and corporations is untrue. Between 1950 and 1980, the top marginal income tax rates for individuals varied from time to time, ranging between 70% and 92%; at the same time, the top marginal income tax rates for corporations ranged between 42% and 52.8%. Compare that to the same rates between 1982 and 2013: 28% to 50% for individuals, and 34% to 46% for corporations. The economy and the middle class grew more during the decades with the higher income tax rates; real wages for workers were higher.

But policies of the past 30 years have taken away much of the balance. The rich end up paying more income taxes because the policies have given them a much larger share of the income, and put more people under the taxable limit for income. Higher taxes on the rich didn't create a situation where the rich pay more income taxes – lower taxes on the rich did. The share of total taxes paid by the rich has gone up due to the rich having a much higher share of the total income, but the share of their income that is taken away in taxes has gone way down, to historically low levels. Policies in Washington have created this situation. Taking away money from those who earn it in order to give it to those who don't earn it? That has already been done. The working class has had their incomes confiscated and given to the very rich.

The concept of "they earn it, so let them keep it" makes little sense when changes in policy have determined who receives it. Why should that concept apply after the policy changes but not before the policy changes?

Whether the wealthy are actually "earning" this redistribution or not, it is going to happen. The fact that it happens is not proof that it is somehow "earned"; the system says it is going to happen anyway. Arguing that it is their money that they have "earned" is a classic circular argument ["They receive it because they earn it". "How do you know that they earn it?" "I know because they receive it"].

The wages paid to workers used to go up when their productivity went up. The economy thrived when that happened. But for the past 30 years, workers' wages have not gone up while the workers' productivity has skyrocketed. This is not some liberal rhetoric. This is not some liberal theory. This is economic fact.

The result of the policies of the past 30 years is that the wealth gap and income gap between the very rich and everybody else are the highest that they have been since just before the Great Depression. We are seeing signs that this is no mere coincidence.

When financial investments earn income for investors, but do not create jobs, they create bubbles instead. These bubbles will eventually burst; guess who pays when they do? Oh, and one more "investment" that contributes to the problem: Political donations to support politicians who promise to maintain this system.

Inequality and Taxes: Makers vs. Takers

(Originally published August 14, 2014 for The Blue Route Blog)

Millions of Americans have been conned into supporting economic policies that work against their own financial interests. These policies also undermine the nation's growth potential and the standard of living that we are capable of achieving. These same policies mean that the American dream of a more prosperous future is attainable for fewer and fewer people.

And how are we being conned? It isn't just with lies and misleading slogans. It isn't just negative rhetoric full of simplistic truisms that appeal to people's baser instincts. Those things are part of it, to be sure. But it is also the selective use of misleading facts combined with some of these truisms, and that is what I want to point out here.

These misleading facts are taken out of context and presented in a way that sounds like they make a valid point. The result is a certain type of invalid argument that sounds valid to those who don't see the context. This type of argument is familiar to us all:

"It isn't fair that the rich (or the 'job creators') are paying all of the taxes while too many people are freeloading. We need to cut the taxes on the rich and make everybody else pay their fair share" "You can't create anything by taking wealth away from those who earn it and give it to those who don't earn it." "If you raise taxes on the rich (and corporations), it will kill jobs. But if you cut taxes on the rich (and corporations), it will create jobs." "Wealth redistribution is unfair because it is taking money from those who earn it and giving it to those who don't earn it." "A flat tax (or a consumption tax) should replace the progressive income tax because it is unfair to tax people more simply because they work harder to earn more." "I support policies that favor the rich because only rich people will give me a job." "It doesn't matter how much income inequality we have because inequality is required in order to provide the necessary incentives for economic growth." "If you complain about inequality, it means that you are jealous of those who have worked hard in order to earn more, and you are engaging in class warfare."

Those are examples of the type of argument that I am talking about. You can probably think of similar ones that I didn't list. The point is that all of these arguments are invalid, even though some facts can be taken out of context and used to support each of these claims. The way to counter such arguments is to take the facts used to support these claims, and put them into proper perspective.

Let's start with these two facts. In the United States we have the least progressive overall tax system since the 1920s, and at the same time we have the most income inequality since the 1920s. A close look at the events and policies that got us to this point will show that those two facts are related. By now you have probably noticed that the current situation is eerily similar to the situation which led up to the Great Depression.

The current income tax rate for the top income brackets is NOT high by historical standards – it is very low, in fact. The arguments that recent problems are created by a stifling tax on "the rich" do not hold up to these facts, especially when you note that during the years of strongest economic growth in our history – in fact the years that the United States became the top economic superpower in the world – the income tax rates at the top were much higher than they are now. It should also be noted that the middle class was created and grew during these years of strong economic growth and higher top-end taxes, but the middle class has shrunk during the most recent years, after the top income tax rates have fallen.

U.S. Top Marginal Tax Rates
1913 - Present

1913-1915	7%		1950-1951	91%
1916	15%		1952-1953	92%
1917	67%		1954-1963	91%
1918	77%		1964	77%
1919-1921	73%		1965-1967	70%
1922-1923	56%		1968	75.25%
1924	46%		1969	77%
1925-1928	25%		1970	71.75%
1929	24%		1971-1980	70%
1930-1931	25%		1981	69.13%
1932-1935	63%		1982-1986	50%
1936-1939	79%		1987	38.5%
1940	81.1%		1988-1990	28%
1941	81%		1991-1992	31%
1942-1943	88%		1993-2000	39.6%
1944-1945	94%		2001	39.1%
1946-1947	86.45%		2002	38.6%
1948-1949	82.13%		2003-2012	35%
			2013-	39.6%

Economics Online Tutor

Not included in the graphic above is the corporate income tax rate, but the history of the corporate rate is similar to the history of the individual rate. For much of the strong growth period of the 1950s, 1960s, and 1970s, the top corporate income tax rate was between 48% and 52%. Since the 1980s, the top corporate income tax rate has been reduced to the current 35%. Again, the historical record does not support the claim that the current income tax rates on the rich and on corporations are stifling the economy.

Federal income tax is only one of many types of tax in the United States. Overall, most taxes historically have been regressive, and the income tax has been progressive to offset this. With the income tax code becoming less and less progressive in recent decades, that balance has been destroyed, and the overall tax code has become flat by historical standards. Those in the top 1/10th of one percent of taxpayers actually pay a little less than those in the top 10%, so at the very high ranges, the income tax becomes regressive. Overall, taxes are only slightly progressive, with taxpayers at all income levels paying an effective rate of around 20% or so to the federal government.

No tax is fair. Any type of tax that favors one group will be considered unfair to another group. Historically, the economy simply worked better when we addressed this "unfairness" issue by having different types of taxes that affected different groups of people with varying degrees of progressiveness – when we had a more progressive income tax structure to offset the regressive nature of other types of taxes. The historical record shows that with a more progressive income tax structure, the income gains in the economy were shared throughout all income levels, even though those with more tended to gain more. Since the income tax rates have become less progressive, however, ALL of the gains have gone to those at the very top of the income levels. For most people, incomes have stagnated and have even decreased in real terms. As a result, the middle class has shrunk and many more people are earning wages at or below poverty levels. Many more people are not able to earn enough to even pay income taxes. More people are without jobs, or require public assistance to supplement their wages.

All of these problems have corresponded to a decrease in the income tax rates for corporations and individuals at the top. I haven't even mentioned that the income tax rates are even less progressive when viewed in terms of effective rates instead of marginal rates, due to an increase in legal loopholes available to corporations and rich individuals.

So here is where we are:

The income tax rates have become much less progressive. In terms of tax rates, the rich pay a much smaller percentage than they have in the past. But the result is that those at the top have received all of the income gains, and everybody else has received none of the gains. More people are working for wages that are less than a living wage. More people are in poverty, and more people need public assistance in order to make ends meet. Put all of these things together, and you have context. You have to be careful not to confuse the total tax rate paid by individual taxpayers, the total tax dollars paid, the income tax rate paid, and the income tax dollars paid.

When a group pays a higher percentage of the total tax DOLLARS, but a much lower percentage in terms of tax RATE, then you know that these people only pay more dollars in their income tax bill because they have more income; no other reason. They are NOT paying more in taxes because of stifling tax rates. They ARE paying more in taxes because lower top end rates have allowed them to receive more of the income. Those who are not paying "their fair share" and are instead receiving "handouts" from those who have to pay more? They are receiving a smaller portion of total national income than they did under a more progressive tax structure. If they had enough income to be taxed, they would be paying taxes. This is an income inequality issue.

If you fall for the con game, you will simply see into this the fact that the rich are paying more of the total tax bill, and more people are receiving "handouts". You will see this as a "makers vs. takers" issue, and of course you will side with the "makers" and blame the "takers". And you would be wrong. You would be failing to see the context. You will fail to see that the situation was created because lower effective tax rates on those at the very top have allowed all of the income growth to stay at the top. You will fail to see that changes in effective tax rates have moved in the opposite direction as changes in total tax dollars, and the change in tax rates has been lower for rich individuals and corporations. The context will tell you what created this situation. The context will also tell you what will fix the situation (hint: do the opposite of what created it). But guess what? Because you have been conned, you will advocate for more of what caused the problem in the first place. You will look at who pays the tax dollars, and advocate for lower rates for these people, even though lower rates for these same people has created the problem. You will be doubling down on failed policies. And it will be so easy for you to blame the victims of all of this – even while you are a victim yourself.

What about wealth redistribution? It has already happened. The rhetoric says otherwise, but the fact is that in the United States today, tax policies ALWAYS redistribute wealth from the poor and middle class to the rich – and from the rich to the super-rich. It NEVER happens the other way around. New wealth that used to go to all of us, wealth that in fact created a large middle class, now all goes to the top. Policies in effect since the 1980s have guaranteed this.

"Taking away from the makers and giving to the takers is unfair." Funny how so many people use that truism to oppose giving even a small portion back to the workers who USED to share in economic growth, but who have had their incomes confiscated by policies which give everything to the rich.

What does this mean for the health of the overall economy?

It means that more and more of the income is going to people who will spend less of it to keep the economy going, supporting domestic businesses, and creating jobs. Income that used to go to people who by necessity would spend most of it supporting domestic businesses and jobs is instead going to people who are taking money out of the real economy in order to "invest" in activities that do not create domestic jobs – activities such as offshore tax havens and financial instruments that are not related to job creation. The lower tax rates on the rich have taken away the incentive to invest in jobs – they don't need the tax write-off that comes from investing in the actual economy if lower income tax rates give them a break anyway.

When financial investments earn income for investors, but do not create jobs, they create bubbles instead. These bubbles will eventually burst, and guess who pays then?

Oh, and one more "investment" that contributes to the problem: Political donations to support politicians who promise to maintain this system.

Why Baseball Stars Make Millions While Teachers Struggle to Survive

(Originally published April 24, 2015 for The Blue Route Blog)

This is a complaint I hear all the time. People from all walks of life complain about it. People from all political persuasions complain about it.

"It isn't fair that some people make millions of dollars every year throwing a ball when those in charge of teaching our children are struggling to survive."

Sometimes, the argument is about movie stars or rock stars instead of sports stars. Sometimes, the argument is about police officers, firefighters, military personnel, or veterans instead of teachers. Sometimes, the argument is about anybody who works hard to scratch out a living instead of public servants. But it's the same argument. Why should entertainers get so much money for possessing unimportant skills when those who do the important and difficult work for us make so little?

And the correct answer is the same in each case. For the answer, we need to look in our collective mirror. That's why this situation exists. That's the ONLY reason this situation exists. The wage discrepancy between entertainers and those of us who work hard and barely get by exists because our collective social values have decided that this is the way it's going to be. Follow the money. The money trail will always tell us what we value as a society.

If you think the solution is for those who pay entertainers big salaries to simply quit paying them so much, think again. The entertainment industry is huge, and expecting it to reallocate its revenue so that its members who happen to be in the public spotlight get less of it won't give more money to teachers, soldiers, firefighters, construction workers, assembly workers, ditch-diggers, and the like. Paying entertainers less would only give more money to the billionaires who have chosen to pay entertainers out of their own pockets.

No, we need to look in the mirror. Our values have determined that this is what the situation is going to be. You might not personally like it. But before you plead innocence while blaming everybody else, you should probably think through this some more.

Do you spend money on sports, movies, popular music, and other entertainment in which the stars make mega-bucks?

Do you buy licensed merchandise or clothing featuring your favorite team, player, or entertainment figure?

Do you support the freedom of other people to choose to spend their money on such things?

Do you watch TV, or support other entertainment media which relies on advertising for revenue?

Do you spend time discussing sports and entertainment with friends, family, and co-workers?

Do you believe that business owners should be able to make their own business decisions?

Do you complain about overpaid government workers?

Are you unwilling to pay more in taxes so that public servants can earn a higher salary?

Do you insist on voting for politicians who won't raise taxes for higher teacher salaries, even if you aren't personally opposed to such taxes?

That covers just about all of us. I can answer "yes" to several of them myself. Perhaps some Amish and a few hermits can be excluded, but they probably won't be reading this. Just about everybody else is covered in this list.

If you answer "yes" to EVEN ONE of these points, then you should look in the mirror. Your values have helped to create this situation. You really shouldn't look for scapegoats.

Of course, there are people among us who don't think this is a problem at all. They answer this complaint with praise for free-market economics, implying that this outcome has been determined by supply and demand and therefore it is a good outcome. In truth, supply and demand play a large role in this outcome, but not as large a role as some people think. There are features specific to the economics of the entertainment industry, and features specific to the economics of public service employment, which vary from the typical supply and demand model. What follows is a brief overview of these features. I'll use baseball players and teachers as examples.

The Economics of Major League Baseball

One fact that people like to bring up about Major League Baseball (MLB) is that it is the ONLY business that has a specific exemption from the Sherman Antitrust Act. No other business, including similar leagues such as the National Football League (NFL), has such an exemption. This fact is not directly related to the financing of baseball vs. the financing of other sports or entertainment businesses. What the exemption means, from a practical standpoint, is that team owners must have permission from the rest of the league in order to move a franchise to a different city. It's why owners of the Dodgers and Giants required permission from other owners to move their baseball teams from New York to California in 1957, but Baltimore Colts owner Robert Irsay was able to sneak his team out of town overnight in 1984 to become the Indianapolis Colts, without permission from the NFL. The ease with which football teams can move due to the fact that the NFL has no anti-trust exemption does mean that football teams have more leverage than baseball teams when it comes to extorting new stadiums and other concessions from local taxpayers. NFL team owners can (and often do) say "pay up or we'll leave town," and rely on sentiment from fans who also happen to be local taxpayers to agree to pay up. Sometimes it works, sometimes it doesn't.

But back to baseball. MLB sets the rules, but each individual team is owned by a corporation, a very rich individual, or a group of rich individuals with a majority owner calling the shots. Teams get revenue from fans going through the turnstiles to watch games in person, but long gone are the days when individual-game ticket sales are the primary source of revenue in baseball.

Many seats at baseball stadiums belong to season-ticket holders. Some season-ticket holders are rich individuals, but many are corporations. Teams put a lot of time and money into wooing corporations to purchase season tickets. Teams also receive revenue from television rights. They get more money if they include corporate-named features in the broadcasts ("and now for the State Farm pitching change"). A few decades ago, teams began fitting stadiums with luxury box suites which generate more money for the teams. A more recent trend has been for teams to sell corporate naming rights to the stadiums themselves. When I was a kid, major league stadiums had names like Candlestick Park, Connie Mack Stadium, Tiger Stadium, Forbes Field, Municipal Stadium, Metropolitan Stadium, and Comiskey Park. The teams which called these stadiums home now play in stadiums which are named AT&T Park, Citizens Bank Park, Comerica Park, PNC Park, Progressive Field, Target Field, and U.S. Cellular Field.

And then there is the shared revenue. Merchandise sales are a big source of revenue. Team logos and the MLB logo are trademarked, and nobody can legally use these logos without league and team permission. If you want a jersey that looks like one worn by your favorite major league player, including the team name and logo, you have to get one licensed by MLB. If you own any such item, take a look at it. It will have the MLB logo on it. You pay for this logo when you buy the merchandise.

The league office at MLB is concerned with competition. Without adequate competition, interest in the games on the field will fall, and so will revenue. This means that smaller-city teams must be able to compete with big-city teams and their much larger fan bases. Team owners have agreed to a rather complex set of revenue-sharing rules to address this issue.

Baseball players get paid according to individual contracts which are within negotiated guidelines. Players making the major league minimum are paid $507,500 per year, but most get paid much more than that. However, only the very best players have major league contracts. Before they are ready to become major-leaguers, players have to pay their dues toiling in the minor leagues. Minor league contracts are not lucrative at all – in fact, many potential stars take themselves out of baseball in order to make a living in the "real" world.

Within these facts of baseball life, team owners are free to run their businesses just like businesses in any other industry. Except that it doesn't always work that way. Baseball differs from free market economics in one important way. For a "normal" business, the goal is to maximize profit. Profit is THE goal. In baseball, profit is only one of the considerations of team owners. It isn't the only consideration. As you might expect, many baseball owners have big egos. Baseball owners might put winning on the field ahead of maximizing the bottom line in an income statement. Think of it this way: Rich people buy yachts. Super rich people buy yachts AND sports teams. Sports teams as well as yachts can be treated as toys by their owners, not as tools for maximizing profits. Team owners can also be motivated by civic pride.

Each team owner is different. They all respond a little differently to these various motivational factors. Some are very business-like and profit-motivated. Some just want to use the team as a way to get their own names in the media. But even the most business-like team owners know that in the long run, profit comes from the fan base, and the fan base is a result of the owners putting together a competitive team. In today's era of free agency – resulting from the removal of baseball's reserve clause which prohibited even unsigned players from negotiating to sell their services to competing teams (thank you, Curt Flood and other pioneers) – players who have fulfilled their contracts can negotiate with other teams, and sign with the highest bidder (within negotiated rules which govern free-agency). This process has driven up player salaries many times over. When a player becomes a free agent, it is said that he is finding his true market value. But is it really "market value" when the ultimate buyer of a player's service is motivated by something other than profit? Yes, for the player, it is market value. But for the finances of baseball itself, it doesn't have to work the same way that "normal" labor markets are supposed to work. The owners who are motivated by winning on the field have an advantage in the free-agent market over owners who just look at the bottom line. Player salaries skyrocketed with the introduction of free agency, but the rate of salary increase has slowed with the introduction of revenue-sharing rules (and in some cases, alleged collusion).

The Economics of Teacher Salaries

Teacher salaries are only marginally related to free market pricing. In order to avoid confusion, I'll make a distinction here between public school teachers and private school teachers. I'll also note that I am talking about K-12 only in this discussion.

Public school teachers are employees of local governments. In fact, teachers comprise more than half of all local government employees nationwide. Funding for local school districts, including funding for teacher salaries, comes from all level of government. Much of the burden for K-12 school funding falls on local – city, and in some cases, county – government. The local budget for schools includes various transfers of funds from other levels of government – mostly the state level, but some funds originate from federal sources. The amount of funds originating from local government sources comprises roughly 35% of all local government budgets nationwide. Funding earmarked for K-12 education is a small amount in the federal budget, a larger amount in the state budget (the states' education budgets are mostly for higher education), and a much larger amount in the local budget.

Local government revenue for education purposes, including teacher salaries, is limited to only a few types of sources. Local governments raise revenue mostly through property taxes, local-option sales taxes, and municipal bonds. Municipal bonds are generally issued for one-time projects such as building construction, and don't tend to figure into budgets for teacher salaries. Municipal bonds also represent a debt that must be repaid by taxpayers at the local level.

Those of us who believe that the teaching profession is underpaid need to ask where the money to correct this situation will come from. Taxpayers don't want their taxes raised. Local budgets are strapped. State budgets are strapped and generally restrained by balanced-budget requirements. The federal government is distanced from local concerns and issues.

Government budgets are strapped. Education spending makes up the largest share of local government spending. Education makes up a large share of state government spending, although the amount that goes to K-12 is much smaller than the single budget item labeled "education" would indicate. Politicians promise to cut budgets wherever they can. This combination of education being a large budget item and politicians looking for budget cuts means that education is usually the first place that state and local governments look for cuts to make. They aren't interested in adding even more money to the budget in order to give teachers more money.

A related side effect, an unfortunate one, is that teachers are victimized by the rhetoric which accompanies the budget-making process in government. Budget cuts are justified using rhetoric which demeans government workers, and teachers are right at the top of the list in terms of a percentage of government workers. Some politicians demean public education altogether. We are told that teachers are overpaid. We are told that teachers make much more than the "average" employee in the private sector, even though the comparisons do not factor in the amount and type of education and training required for each profession. Teachers unions are blamed for the "high" cost of teacher salaries. Experienced teachers are being called "bad teachers" in attempts to replace them with younger and less experienced teachers – and to decrease the average salary of teachers. Real and perceived problems with the results of our education system are being blamed on individual teachers. Many education reform efforts are based on this rhetoric.

What about increasing funding at the federal level in order to take the burden off local property-tax payers as well as state and local governments? This shifting of tax burden means that somebody still has to pay, but it can be justified under the American principle of "equal opportunity" (do kids who live in school districts which include rich property owners deserve a better education than everybody else?) and the importance of education as a part of our infrastructure – even as a part of national interest. But there is a conflict between local control of education on the one hand, and the national interests on the other hand. How much control over school policy should be given to the federal government? This conflict cannot be resolved through the application of prevailing economic theory.

What about private education? If teacher salaries in the public sector depend on taxpayers, politicians, and government budgets, what about teachers in the private sector? Should education be privatized in order to eliminate education spending from government budgets altogether?

The answer to that last question is an emphatic "NO!" First of all, you can't increase teacher salaries simply by adding in a profit motive to those who pay teachers, unless there is a way to structure education so that higher salary expenses will lead to higher profits.

But there is a much bigger reason why privatization of education is a very bad idea. Ask yourself these two questions:

What is the purpose of education?

What is the purpose of a private, for-profit company?

If you answer those two questions, you should be able to see very easily that the goals of education are not compatible with the goals of private industry.

One final reality which separates teacher salaries from other salaries in terms of supply and demand: The supply of workers for specific jobs outside the field of education depends on advantages which the job offers to potential employees – things like salary; benefits, working conditions, and opportunity. A ditch-digger isn't normally someone who thinks his purpose in life, his God-given calling to serve, is to dig ditches. But many teachers do indeed feel such an obligation to teach. This means that in a comparison of the teaching profession to nearly every other profession, the supply of labor for teachers is artificially high, driving down wages. (If you disagree with that last statement because you observe a teacher shortage, you are confusing the supply of teachers with the quantity of teachers supplied at the prevailing salary.)

Is it "fair" that entertainers and sports stars get paid so much more than those who do society's vital work? Our collective system of values says that this is the way it will be. If we are okay with the outcome, we probably will say that the system is fair. If we aren't okay with the outcome, then perhaps we should reexamine our values. But in order to do that, each of us needs to look in the mirror instead of pointing fingers elsewhere.

Section 4: The Role of Corporations in the Economy

Corporations and the Public Interest: Lessons from History

(Originally published September 23, 2015 for The Blue Route Blog)

"A corporation is an artificial being, invisible, intangible, and existing only in contemplation of law. Being the mere creature of law, it possesses only those properties which the charter of its creation confers upon it." ~ Chief Justice John Marshall, *Dartmouth College v. Woodward, 1819*

*

Here is a fact to think about. The corporation is something that the government has created. When you consider the implications of corporate personhood, start at the beginning. The government created the corporate structure, and every organization within the corporate structure owes its existence to the government. If a corporation is a person, then the government is its parent.

A corporation can only exist because we have laws that say it can exist. A corporate charter granted by the government is a license for the corporation to exist. The corporate structure isn't something that is inherent in nature. It also is not mandatory. Organizations choose to incorporate, because the laws passed by the government make it beneficial for them to do so. Legal benefits of incorporation include preferential tax treatment as well as certain types of limited liability. The only reason an organization will choose a legal corporate structure is because the benefits of doing so – benefits granted by the government – are perceived to outweigh the benefits of alternative organizational structures. The government, and nobody else, has provided organizations with alternatives; one of which is legal incorporation.

Why does the government agree to this setup? To put the question another way: If the government belongs to We the People, why would we as a people agree to this? What benefits do we receive?

The simple answer is: We the People, through our government, have decided that the existence of the corporate structure is good for the economy and good for society.

We can cite some economic theories to back up this claim: the benefits of the corporate structure provide incentives which make the economy more efficient.

We can even pick out some facts to back up this claim: corporations provide millions of our jobs, and corporations provide many of the technological advances that we enjoy.

If we take a closer look at this, we can find some important truths in such claims. We should not ignore these truths; however, the same closer look will reveal that these claims do not tell the whole story.

If We the People, through our government, are responsible for the existence of corporations, then We the People, through our government, have the right to insist that the actions of corporations are in the public interest. Corporations exist for our benefit, and we have a right to make sure that they act accordingly. Indeed, our elected officials have a duty to see to it that corporations are acting in the public interest. The government provides the legal structure in order for corporations to exist. We have absolutely no reason to allow corporations to use the benefits we give them in a way that undermines the public good. After all, we created corporations so that we can benefit from their existence, and for no other reason.

If you think that corporations always, or nearly always, act in the public interest, then you haven't been paying attention. If you think that we have to accept the status quo, and all of its negative outcomes, on the grounds that the positive outweighs the negative, then you don't understand the social costs and public options involved. A full explanation of these points would fill volumes, and be far beyond the scope of this essay. But if you take a look at the history of corporations in America, you should be able to understand the serious problems faced by our society due to corporate actions that are not in the public interest. You will see that it hasn't always been this way, and that it doesn't have to be this way.

I won't attempt to list and explain all of these problems. I couldn't do justice to the subject in the length of an essay. Instead, my approach will be to let the historical record speak for itself. What follows is a brief history of corporations in America.

*

The United States was formed in large part out of distrust of corporate power. The dominance of British corporations over everyday life in the colonies, and the powers granted to these corporations by the British government through corporate money's influence in Parliament, provided the economic reasons for the American Revolution. The Boston Tea Party was a revolt against corporations having so much power that the people had become economic slaves to the dictates of corporations.

Real life experience with corporations such as the British East India Company left the American colonists with a strong distrust of corporations and corporate power. This distrust carried over to the men who wrote the founding documents, including the Constitution. The founders knew that the concentration of wealth and political power through large corporations could not coexist with personal freedom and self-determination.

The American founders left the power to grant corporate charters to the individual states in order to put corporations under tight local control. The distrust of corporations was widespread throughout the populace and throughout the states, and states placed severe restrictions on corporate charters. If you think the regulation of corporations is overbearing today, check out how corporate power was limited at the time of America's founding, and for nearly 100 years afterward:

Corporations were viewed as a necessary evil, and charters initially were granted only for purposes of providing the national infrastructure.

State legislators debated each charter application.

Very few corporate charters were granted.

Corporate restrictions were often included in state constitutions as well as state laws.

Corporate charters were granted for a limited time and for a limited purpose.

Corporate charters specified which activities each corporation was allowed to engage in.

Corporate activities were limited to one purpose only.

Corporations were forbidden from owning property that wasn't necessary meet a specified and approved purpose.

Corporations were required to justify that their activities were in the public interest.

Corporate ownership of stock in other companies was prohibited.

Corporate mergers were forbidden.

Corporate owners and managers were held criminally responsible for crimes committed by corporations.

The penalty for corporate misconduct was dissolution and liquidation of the corporation.

Corporations were not allowed to make political contributions or spend money in an attempt to influence legislation.

Corporate size was often limited by law.

Corporate debts were often limited by law.

Corporate profits were sometimes limited by law.

Legislators could audit corporate records at any time.

Small shareholders had equal voting rights with large shareholders.

Corporate directors could not serve more than one company.

That's the way it was at the time of the founding of the United States, and for nearly 100 years afterward. The corporation existed to serve the public interest. There were no conglomerates. There were no giant multi-national corporations. There was no concept of corporate personhood. Corporations did not own the government, hire lobbyists, or spend money in attempts to increase their political or economic power through legislation.

The idea that corporations are **not** people, and that they exist only to serve the public interest, was commonplace within the court system as well as the general public.

"A corporation can have no legal existence out of the boundaries of the sovereignty by which it is created. It exists only in contemplation of law and by force of the law. … It is indeed a mere artificial being." ~ Chief Justice Roger Taney, *Bank of Augusta v. Earle, 1839*

*

As you can see, this picture of early corporations in America is a far cry from today's reality. What happened in the meantime?

During the American Civil War, corporations were granted large contracts to support war efforts. Many corporations took advantage of wartime chaos and ignored limitations imposed on them by their charters. Corporate wealth began to grow. Some corporations made money from both sides in the war. Bribery of government officials was commonplace, as was price gouging on government contracts.

"We may congratulate ourselves that this cruel war is nearing its end. It has cost a vast amount of treasure and blood ... It has indeed been a trying hour for the Republic; but I see in the near future a crisis approaching that unnerves me and causes me to tremble for the safety of my country. As a result of war, corporations have been enthroned and an era of corruption in high places will follow, and the money power of the country will endeavor to prolong its reign by working upon the prejudices of the people until all wealth is aggregated in a few hands, and the Republic is destroyed. I feel at this moment more anxiety for the safety of my country than ever before, even in the midst of war. God grant that my suspicions may prove groundless."~ President Abraham Lincoln, letter to Col. William F Elkins dated November 21, 1864

*

In the years and decades following the Civil War, federal courts (including the U.S. Supreme Court) often ruled in favor of corporations in charter disputes with states. As a result, corporations began to test their limits and assume more power in violation of charter agreements.

The new support from the court system, combined with the advent of the Industrial Revolution and continued western settlement, led to widespread exploitation of workers. Company towns sprang up in numerous places. Labor organizers were blacklisted. The Industrial Revolution meant that many people who used to be self-employed farmers, merchants, and craftsmen – as well as those who had worked for local employers who were answerable to the community – were suddenly dependent on absentee corporate owners for a paycheck. The threat of unemployment meant that these workers were easy to exploit.

In addition to exploiting workers, corporations began exploiting their new-found legal victories by ignoring many different charter restrictions. They began to form conglomerations and trusts. They spent freely on obtaining favors from politicians. They purchased newspapers which published pro-corporate and anti-labor rhetoric in order to gain public support for corporate power. Wealth and power were removed from local communities and given to absentee corporate owners.

In 1886, the U.S. Supreme Court ruled in *Santa Clara County v. Southern Pacific Railroad* that a corporation was a "natural person". After that ruling, corporations increasingly asserted more personhood rights under the 14th Amendment to the Constitution, an amendment enacted for the purpose of protecting the rights to freed slaves. Since that time, judges have routinely struck down laws restricting corporate activities on the grounds that corporate personhood is protected by the 14th Amendment. Thus began the concept of "corporations are people" – and the era of corporate money in politics.

"As we view the achievements of aggregated capital, we discover the existence of trusts, combinations, and monopolies, while the citizen is struggling far in the rear, or is trampled beneath an iron heel. Corporations, which should be the carefully restrained creatures of the law and the servants of the people, are fast becoming the people's masters." ~ President Grover Cleveland, 1888

*

The rights that courts granted to corporations through the 14th Amendment often came with limits. It wasn't until 1978, in *First National Bank of Boston v. Bellotti*, that the U.S. Supreme Court ruled that 1st Amendment free speech rights included the right for corporations to spend money to influence political outcomes.

In 2010's *Citizens United v. Federal Election Commission*, the U.S. Supreme Court ruled that corporate 1st Amendment rights to free speech, as defined by money spent to influence the political process, was unlimited.

The Citizens United ruling means that...

1. Political favors go to the highest bidder.

2. Those with the most money are entitled to the most protection under the 1st Amendment.

3. The Supreme Court has made a mockery of American history, including the preamble to the Declaration of Independence, the justification for the American Revolution, and the original meaning of the very Constitution that the Court is sworn to uphold.

4. Political power that goes to those with the most money has replaced the democratic principle that each citizen has equal power and equal opportunity.

5. Economic inequality is increasing – solely because of laws written to serve the moneyed interests.

6. Decisions which affect the livelihoods of the populace are being made behind closed doors by unelected corporate executives.

7. Moneyed interests control much of the information available to the people.

8. The legality of corporate personhood is complete.

9. Candidates for political office must spend a lot of money in order to get elected, and the only way they can get the amount of money necessary is by serving the needs of the moneyed interests (namely corporations) rather than serving the needs of We the People, as established by the Constitution.

10. We the People are not entitled to see the names of those who are bankrolling our political system.

11. The government has been rendered legally powerless to control the amount of money in politics.

12. Due to corporate personhood and money in politics, government officials must serve corporate interests.

13. We the People must serve the interests of corporations which have been created by our laws to serve us.

14. Corporations no longer have a responsibility to serve the public interest.

Other than waiting for a future Supreme Court with a different majority to take up a relevant case and reverse this ruling, there is no way to undo the damage caused by Citizens United – unless enough people become educated on the subject so that a constitutional amendment reversing this ruling can receive the necessary support from a cross-section of Americans.

"Our aim is not to do away with corporations; on the contrary, these big aggregations are an inevitable development of modern industrialism, and the effort to destroy them would be futile unless accomplished in ways that would work the utmost mischief to the entire body politic. We can do nothing of good in the way of regulating and supervising these corporations until we fix clearly in our minds that we are not attacking the corporations, but endeavoring to do away with any evil in them. We are not hostile to them; we are merely determined that they shall be so handled as to serve the public good. We draw the line against misconduct, not against wealth." ~ President Theodore Roosevelt, State of the Union Address 1902

*

Corporations are people? The government is the parent to these corporate persons?

Flesh-and-blood parents exist for the benefit of their flesh-and-blood children. We are supposed to want what is best for our children. We chase the American Dream, and hope that our children have a better, more prosperous life than we have. We serve their needs. But governments do not exist for the benefit of corporations. Governments exist for the benefit of We the People. Governments created corporations, not for the purpose of having the government serve corporations, but for the purpose of having corporations serve the interests of the people. The entire concept of corporate personhood turns logic on its head.

Unfortunately, a majority of the current U.S. Supreme Court has ruled otherwise.

Corporate-Style Profit Maximization is Harming the Economy

(Originally published April 1, 2015 for The Blue Route Blog)

One of the basic tenets in the teaching of economics is that the goal of a business is to maximize profit. Economic theories and concepts hinge on the idea that all activities and decisions made by entrepreneurs and managers of for-profit organizations are motivated by profit-maximization.

Businesses earn revenue. In doing so, they hire factors of production (land, labor, capital). These factors impose costs on the businesses. The goal of a business is to maximize profit which mathematically is equal to revenue minus cost. This is basic economics. It is also basic accounting.

According to the teaching of economic theory, the idea that all business decisions are based on the profit-maximizing motive is not only good for the economy, but it is also a vital part of the benefits of having a market-based economy. Profit sends out the necessary signals for reallocating resources. Without these signals generated by the profit motive, resources will not be allocated efficiently. Consumers will suffer. The standard of living will be below its potential.

If a company makes widgets, then its business decisions will be based on a determination of which combination of resources will earn the company the most profit through the sale of widgets. Management will have to decide how many widgets to make, which combination of inputs to use, where to get the inputs, what kind of trade-off between quality and cost to use, how to market the product, and much more. These are the types of decisions which can vary from one company to another, even from one manager to another. But they are all based on the underlying motive of maximizing profit through the manufacture and sale of widgets.

This profit-maximizing motive in turn creates more economic efficiency in the economy. The company itself will earn more profit if it allocates its resources with more efficiency. The industry and the overall economy will both become more efficient through signals generated by existing profits. Profit-seekers will leave less-efficient industries and instead put resources into more-efficient industries. As long as more profit can be made by doing something different, then profit-seekers will choose to do something different. An industry with large profits will attract more competitors, which will reduce the profits of individual companies until the motivation to enter the industry is gone. An industry with losses will have businesses leaving the industry, as profit-seekers move into more profitable activities. An industry will be in equilibrium only when each company makes enough profit so that it can remain in business without being motivated to leave, but not so much profit that it attracts more competition. At that point, efficiency will be reached.

The part in the last paragraph about "enough profit so that it can remain in business" means that a certain amount of profit is necessary for each company. The concept of "normal profit" comes into play. Normal profit is the amount of profit required to maintain equilibrium, and therefore is a cost of doing business. The equation "profit equals revenue minus cost" is an accounting equation. When you add normal profit to the cost side, the mathematical result of the equation is called economic profit. Equilibrium exists when economic profit is zero. If economic profit is negative, then this signals that resources will be allocated elsewhere, and that businesses will leave the industry. Negative economic profit indicates that resource allocation is inefficient, and a reallocation will occur. If economic profit is positive, then this signals that more resources will be allocated into the industry, and that businesses will enter the industry. Positive economic profit also indicates that resource allocation is inefficient, and a reallocation will occur. Only when economic profit is zero will efficiency and equilibrium result.

Those are the basic points of the theory behind the role that profit plays in the economy. I provided a short version of this theory in order to better illustrate my main point, which is that the role of profit for corporations has been divorced from the benefits of economic efficiency to a large degree.

Profit is equal to revenue minus cost. Business decisions are based on attempts to maximize this equation. A widget manufacturer will be motivated to maximize the bottom line on an income statement.

But this is not true if the widget manufacturer happens to have a corporate structure. The bottom line on an income statement is a factor, but it is not the only factor. You will note that the theory of efficiency requires ALL business decisions to be directed towards that bottom line. But for corporations, this is different.

You might think of profit as being the bottom line on an income statement, and the basic theory of efficiency would agree with you. But corporations don't think that way. To a corporation, profit means "shareholder value." A corporation is NOT motivated to maximize accounting profit on an income statement. A corporation IS motivated to maximize shareholder value.

That's right. The sole purpose of any corporation is to manipulate stock prices.

There is a theoretical basis for this. You can even find that theory in economics textbooks. The theory is that for a corporation, the business itself is a mythical entity which owns nothing, and earns no profit. The stockholders are the ones who own everything. Maximizing stockholder return IS what corporate profit is all about. (I'm not sure how this theory supports the notion of corporate personhood).

The term "maximizing profit" is rather loosely defined in economic theory. For one thing, it can refer to activities designed to increase current profits; or it can refer to activities which reduce current profits in favor of future profits. Different competitors within the same industry can operate under different ideas of what "profit" means to them, yet economic theory says that each has the same goal of maximizing profit. In the corporate world, changing this definition to "maximizing shareholder value" encompasses a whole new set of business activities.

Theory aside, what is the real-world result of equating profit with shareholder value rather than with the income statement?

As I said above, the bottom line on the income statement is part of the equation. But it isn't the only part. Corporate decision-makers are free to do just about anything that they can justify as "maximizing shareholder value." Increasingly, they are using their resources on things that are not related to the income statement. Increasingly, they are making corporate decisions which do not contribute to the economy's efficiency or the overall standard of living. To put it another way, corporate decisions are increasingly divorced from the production of widgets.

Take a look at corporate newsmakers. Read the financial pages. What are these news stories about? What are corporations making news for? Are they in the news because of operating profits? Is it for activities which contribute to the overall economy? Or are they in the news for activities directly related to the manipulation of stock prices? Is the money going into the "real" economy, or is it contributing to a stock market bubble?

Mergers, divestitures, stock buy-backs, tax inversions, lawsuits, lobbying congress, lobbying stockbrokerage firms, and using the media to spread propaganda are just a few of the activities which corporations are increasingly engaged in – activities not necessarily related directly to the production of widgets, so to speak. Some of these activities can actually be justified under economic theory. Do the activities increase or decrease competition and its resulting effects on the efficiency of the economy? Perhaps a decrease in competition can be justified as an increase in economies of scale. But the theory only works in the real world under specific circumstances. The theory probably doesn't apply for activities which are conducted with only the effects on stock prices in mind.

What about corporate campaign spending? Does anybody believe that corporations finance political campaigns out of a sense of patriotism, willing to sacrifice billions of dollars with no thought of receiving a return on this investment? Or is it more likely that they are telling politicians that if they want to get elected, the politicians had better provide corporations with a healthy return on the investment?

And how, exactly, is campaign spending going to help corporations to produce widgets?

Section 5: The Role of Government in the Economy

Life, Liberty, and the Pursuit of Happiness

(Originally published August 4, 2014 for The Blue Route Blog)

"We hold these truths to be self-evident, that all men are created equal, that they are endowed by their Creator with certain unalienable Rights, that among these are Life, Liberty and the pursuit of Happiness. — That to secure these rights, Governments are instituted among Men, deriving their just powers from the consent of the governed, — That whenever any Form of Government becomes destructive of these ends, it is the Right of the People to alter or to abolish it, and to institute new Government, laying its foundation on such principles and organizing its powers in such form, as to them shall seem most likely to effect their Safety and Happiness."

*

These famous words are in the preamble to the Declaration of Independence, written over 238 years ago. I see in these words a blueprint for society, a blueprint for human progress. The words themselves represent ideals that we have never reached, and perhaps imperfect humans could never reach. Thomas Jefferson, the author, fell far short of living up to his own words. We certainly have not attained perfection according to the ideals in the 238 years that have passed since these words were written.

But that is what we get when we use ideals as a blueprint. We have always fallen short; perhaps we always will, but that doesn't mean that we should give up. We always have something to work towards. What I see in the historical record is this:

Events and outcomes that bring us closer to the ideals expressed in these words reflect progress of society, progress of humankind. Events and outcomes that take us further away from the ideals expressed in these words reflect societal and human regression.

It would be foolish to focus on historical failings instead of the lessons to be learned. Certainly there are lessons to be learned here. We ignore the lessons when we dismiss these words by pointing out the failings of the author or the type of society that he helped to create. We ignore the lessons when we become satisfied with advances we have made instead of trying to understand what still needs to be done. Perhaps it would help if we understood the word "men" in the phrase "all men are created equal" as a term relating to humankind, not as a masculine term.

This is the blueprint that I am referring to:

"All men are created equal", and "they are endowed by their Creator with certain unalienable Rights". "Governments are instituted among Men" "to secure these rights". Society regresses "whenever any Form of Government becomes destructive to these ends".

Some people refer to these "unalienable rights" as natural rights. The ideals that I refer to are the attainment of these rights, the protection of these rights, and the guarantee that all people and all groups of people are universally acknowledged to possess these rights as equals. The fact that we have not reached these ideals as a society means that in order to advance we need to treat these words as a blueprint.

Unalienable rights – specifically life, liberty, and the pursuit of happiness – take precedence over everything else in society. We may consider these rights to be natural, but we do not retain them in the absence of a government "to secure these rights". The historical record is very clear on this. Humans do not retain rights, and are not treated as equals, without the presence of a government "to secure these rights". Also, humans do not retain rights, and are not treated as equals, if the government "becomes destructive to these ends". It is up to us, as citizens, to ensure that the government understands that it derives its "just powers from the consent of the governed", and governs accordingly. When the government fails to do so, it is our duty to make whatever changes are necessary.

We must make sure that we have a government that is there to secure our rights. We must keep in mind that such a government is there to treat all people as equals. It is not there to protect "my" rights by taking rights away from other people. It is not there to treat some groups of people as being second-class citizens. It is not there to allow some people to use their wealth to control the distribution of rights. "All men are created equal". Unless we understand this, we will not be able to make progress as a society.

Our government does not have rights.

Our institutions do not have rights.

Laws are not rights.

Law enforcement is not a right.

Even military protection is not a right.

These are nothing more than tools for securing these rights: "Life, Liberty, and the pursuit of Happiness."

If these tools are used for something other than securing these rights for everyone, then they are being misused. If these tools are used for something that runs counter to these rights, then they must be stopped, and if necessary abolished in the name of humanity.

Keynesian Economics, Government, and Budget Deficits

(Originally published December 1, 2014 for The Blue Route Blog)

"Let Pharaoh do this, and let him appoint officers over the land, and take up the fifth part of the land of Egypt in the seven plenteous years. And let them gather all the food of those good years that come, and lay up corn under the hand of Pharaoh, and let them keep food in the cities. And that food shall be for store to the land against the seven years of famine, which shall be in the land of Egypt; that the land perish not through the famine." ~ Genesis 41: 34-36, KJV

*

Whatever your beliefs, I recommend that you read Genesis 41. It contains important lessons for modern-day economics.

Genesis 41 is the story of Joseph interpreting Pharaoh's dreams about a famine which is to come. Joseph's advice to Pharaoh, depicted in the narrative as being extremely wise, was to save the people of Egypt through the use of Keynesian economics. Of course, that terminology isn't found in the story – it would be thousands of years before Keynes would come along. But the actions advised by Joseph and Keynesian economics use the same principles. Joseph advised Pharaoh to take up a tax during the good years as a protection against the consequences of the inevitable bad years to come. You might not recognize that this is an ancient description of modern-day Keynesian economics. Rather than being a modern liberal scheme, Keynesian economic concepts can be traced all the way back to the Torah – all the way back to the very first book of the Bible.

Keynesian economics is widely misunderstood. Arguments against its use tend to be straw man arguments against a misunderstood concept of Keynesian economics. This misunderstanding has been compounded by additions and alterations to economic theory as well as the creation of new branches of economic schools of thought by those who call themselves Keynesians. When I use the term "Keynesian economics", I am specifically referencing the concepts taught by John Maynard Keynes, and not the concepts added over the years by neo-Keynesians and others.

John Maynard Keynes' writing is somewhat difficult to read, especially for those who are untrained at reading text regarding economics concepts and theory. According to classical economic theory, an economic collapse as deep and as lengthy as the Great Depression could not possibly occur – yet it did occur. According to classical theory, the economy would very quickly correct for such a collapse – yet that correction did not occur. Perhaps the correction would have come eventually. But during the depths of the Great Depression, it was clear that we couldn't afford to wait for "eventually" to get here. Along came Keynes, with a new theory to explain…

…why the Great Depression occurred

…what the government could do to fix it

…how to deal with economic downturns in the future

…how to prevent future catastrophic economic events

Since this was a new theory to replace a prevailing-yet-now-debunked theory, Keynes needed to include a lot of details in his writing; details which served to put an understanding of his writing beyond the reach of the general population.

Perhaps these details hide the basic principles behind Keynesian economics and help lead to confusion. The basic points are:

1. Economic collapses beyond an acceptable level are possible.

2. The government can make these collapses less catastrophic, less frequent, and shorter in length through fiscal policies, which are policies involving taxing and government spending.

3. This involves using gains earned during good economic times to pay for the bad economic times.

These basic points are often misunderstood because they can hide behind the details and the rhetoric.

Classical economic theory had been debunked by the reality of the Great Depression. Those who initially opposed Keynesian methods were, for the most part, not classical economists but Monetarists. Monetarists believed that fiscal policies were riskier and perhaps less effective than monetary policies involving government intervention in interest rates and the money supply. Monetarists tended to be conservatives who would avoid the use of fiscal policies as tools to influence the economy, and instead use a consistent monetary policy which should only be changed in the direst of circumstances. The leader of the Monetarist movement was the conservative economist Milton Friedman.

Today's liberal economic policies have generally descended from Keynes while today's conservative economic policies have generally descended from Friedman. These are only generalizations, however, and are based more on the historic timeline of policy changes than on adherence to original theories. Conservative rhetoric today often seems to be more in line with the debunked classical theories than with the original Monetarists.

There are liberal advocates who claim that Keynesian economics has never actually been attempted in the United States, at least not to the extent that Keynes advocated. The New Deal is generally thought to be a massive Keynesian departure from anything previously attempted. Keynesian economics provided a justification for such a departure. Yet Keynes and Roosevelt did not see eye to eye on economic policy. To Keynes, the New Deal did not provide enough of a jolt to the economy. It wasn't big enough, and its stimulus policies were abandoned long before full recovery.

Conservative rhetoric includes a number of misconceptions regarding Keynesian economics. I want to mention a few of these misconceptions:

1. Contrary to the rhetoric, Keynesian economics is not socialism, and it is not "big government". It is simply using the gains from good economic times in order to avoid the worst consequences of bad economic times through fiscal policy. Keynes had been, and remained, a free-market advocate.

2. Keynesian economics cannot be blamed for long-term growth in the national debt. On the contrary, long term deficits which increase the debt are created through deficit spending during good economic times. Budget deficits during good economic times run counter to Keynes' philosophy. Keynesian deficits are recession-fighting tools, not a normal way of economic life. John Maynard Keynes was very upset with Roosevelt for massive government debts incurred for war efforts. To Keynes' way of thinking, if there is not enough of a surplus built up to pay for hard economic times, then short term deficits are preferable to widespread pain and suffering – we will just cover these deficits when economic times improve. Eliminating pain and suffering through the use of surpluses is preferable to deficit spending, but short term deficits are preferable to allowing widespread pain and suffering. You can think of government surpluses as a rainy day fund. The Great Recession which officially began in December of 2007 and the deficits which resulted from it were made much worse because a

budget surplus had been squandered on inappropriate tax cuts and unpaid-for war efforts. If the surplus had still existed in 2007, the steps necessary to end the recession would have involved less public deficit spending.

3. Contrary to the rhetoric, Keynesian economic policies are Constitutional and are consistent with the intent of the Founding Fathers, even if the same Founding Fathers could not possibly anticipate such changes to prevailing academic thought regarding economics.

Prior to Keynes, the idea of using government policy to influence economic outcomes was alien to most economists. After Keynes, this same idea became encoded in federal law. The Employment Act of 1946 requires the government to make policy for the purpose of generating full employment while maintaining price stability. This law has no real teeth: It doesn't define how the government is supposed to do this; it doesn't specify which policies to use; it doesn't provide for direction when the twin goals of employment and price stability clash; and it doesn't specify measures of success. But it is law, and both fiscal and monetary policies have been implemented for the same purposes that the law was created for. This law implies that activist economic policies should be used not only after the economy has gone into recession, but also to prevent recessions in the first place. Activism to prevent economic instability caused by price fluctuations is also implied.

What is the government's track record for meeting the terms of the Employment Act of 1946? Has the government succeeded in generating employment while maintaining price stability? Let's compare the record before interventionist policies with the record since these policies have been used. The data clearly shows that overall, economic stability has increased – not decreased – with these policies. Perhaps we can all disagree with specific policies at specific points in time, but I think the overall track record is quite impressive. How much of the increase in stability that can be credited to…

…automatic stabilizers and other recession-related Keynesian policies

…activist monetary policies through the Federal Reserve

…elimination of a gold standard

…other factors

are questions that are open to debate. But the track record is very clear. The United States' economy has become much more stable with activist policies.

Avoiding Recessions

Recessions involve widespread unemployment. The state of the economy coming out of a recession is always at a lower point than it was going in. Recessions have become less frequent, shorter in length, and less severe than they were prior to the Employment Act of 1946.

Recessions have become less frequent:

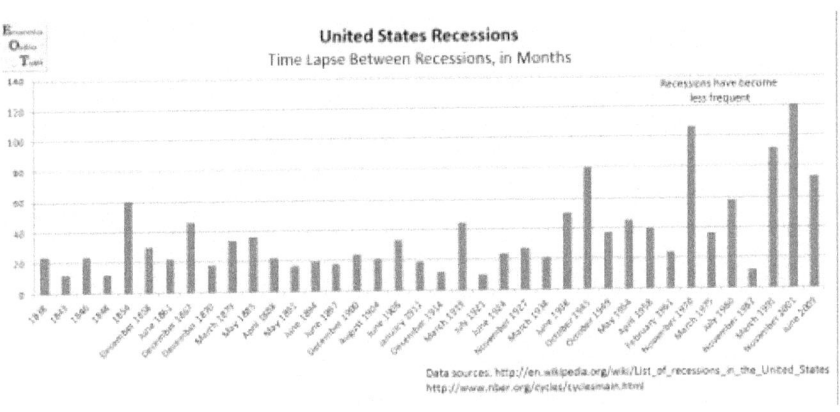

Recessions have become shorter in length:

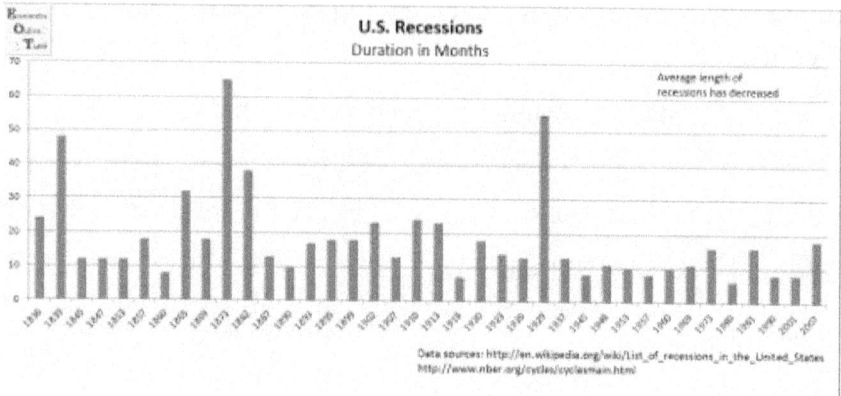

Recessions have become less severe:

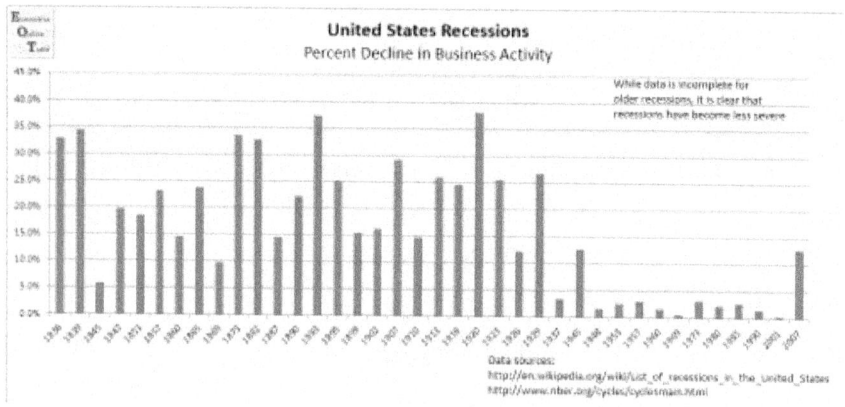

What about stable prices?

Overall, prices have become more stable. For the most part, inflation has been high enough to avoid the dire consequences of deflation. Inflation has largely stayed in the range considered by most economists as being consistent with economic growth. Despite numerous predictions of doom over the years, inflation has never approached anything close to hyperinflation. Except for events related to the Arab oil embargo of the1970s, inflation has rarely topped 5% per year. The last time we had an inflation rate above 5% for an entire year was 1990, at 5.4%. The last year of double-digit inflation was 1981, at 10.3%.

What about a trade-off between inflation and unemployment?

The historical data does not support a claim that such a trade-off exists under normal circumstances.

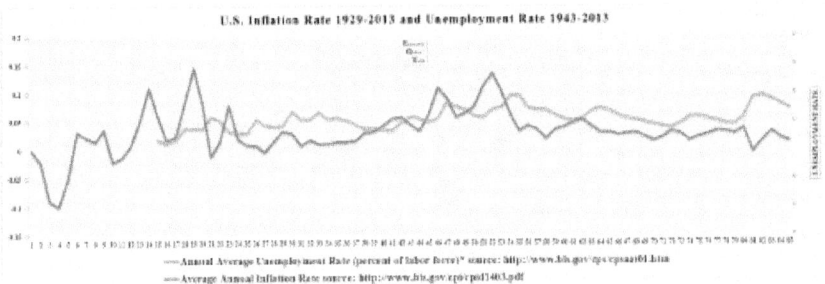

U.S. Inflation Rate 1929-2013 and Unemployment Rate 1943-2013

The story of Joseph and Pharaoh was set in ancient times involving an ancient economic system. Modern-day economic methods and tools are much different. The tax imposed by Pharaoh actually involved the government confiscating land from the private sector, in order for the government to claim ownership of a 20% tax on crops. Today, our economy is much more complex, and tax involves payment of money rather than land and crops.

Keynesian-type policies allow for short term debt to be part of the process, if necessary. But government debt can certainly exist outside of any anti-recession policy. Long term debt always does. It does not follow logically, or economically, that the availability of government debt as part of fiscal policy for fighting recessions means that all government debt is caused by Keynesian economic policies.

Ignore the rhetoric, and check the record. Short term government debt created in fighting the consequences of recessions is sometimes necessary for the stability of the overall economy, as well as the well-being of individual citizens. We have numerous automatic stabilizers in place which serve these purposes. A balanced budget amendment, even if it is well-intentioned, would undermine the entire economy. It takes an understanding of the difference between deficits created for economic stabilization (short term, or cyclical, deficits) and deficits created for other purposes such as war or to provide tax breaks (long term, or structural, deficits).

The former are Keynesian deficits; the latter are not.

Fences and Regulations

(Originally published February 28, 2015 for The Blue Route Blog)

"Don't ever take a fence down until you know why it was put up." ~ Robert Frost

*

Be careful what you wish for. Business regulations exist to benefit businesses as well as customers, employees, and public health & safety. Regulations are necessary for a stable economy.

Without regulations, it is likely that entire industries would not exist, and other industries would have far fewer customers. More employees would die simply because they were trying to earn a living. The overall economy would be much smaller. Perhaps the United States economy would look more like the self-sufficiency of the pioneer and Wild West days – for good and for bad – than today's global economic powerhouse.

However, we are all very much aware that compliance is costly – so much so that deregulation is a popular position for politicians. According to deregulatory rhetoric, all regulations are "anti-business". This rhetoric is wrong, and deregulation for its own sake is misguided. Regulations provide a stable business environment, complete with enhancing consumer confidence.

And yet, regulations are costly, so the anti-regulatory movement continues. While it is true that deregulation for its own sake is misguided, it is also true that regulation for its own sake is misguided. Are regulations placing too much of a burden on businesses and the economy? Probably, at least in certain areas, but given the benefits which regulations provide to businesses, the answer isn't as clear-cut as the rhetoric would lead you to believe. Are some regulations misguided or at least outdated? I'm sure that the answer is "yes". Are there redundancies and other inefficiencies in our system of regulation? The answer to that one is also "yes".

Here is where the analogy of fences comes into the discussion.

Keep in mind that existing regulations were created for specific reasons. Each regulation has a history, and a reason to exist. Perhaps that reason no longer applies; perhaps that reason wasn't a good reason in the first place. Remember, though, that businesses rely on regulations for customers, employees, and a stable economic environment – whether or not these businesses are aware of the benefits of regulations.

The point that I am trying to make is this: When we eliminate regulations for the sole purpose of having fewer regulations – with no regard for the purpose that each regulation was created in the first place – we get results that are disastrous.

Deregulation as a policy does not have a very good track record. Financial meltdowns, deep recessions, wage stagnation and other problems have been associated with deregulation. The reason for this can be seen in the fences analogy. We are told it isn't wise to tear down fences unless we know why they were put up in the first place. In the same way, we shouldn't eliminate regulations until we understand why they exist in the first place. Each regulation was put into place for its own reason. Whether or not that reason currently is valid can only be determined by weighing each regulation on its own merits. What are the effects, good and bad, of having a specific regulation in place? What would be the effects of eliminating that specific regulation?

Yes, regulations are costly. Yes, regulations can be misguided, outdated, or redundant. But at the same time, some regulations are necessary, and eliminating them could have disastrous results.

How, then, to we get rid of "bad" regulations? It's easy to go along with the political rhetoric, and support deregulation for its own sake, in order to show that we are "pro-business." That would be the simple (simplistic) way, but it would be misguided. Another way would be to allow businesses and industries to regulate themselves. But that policy also has a poor track record. Just to cite a couple of examples, take a look at the salmonella-from-eggs scare of 2010 or the 2013 West, Texas fertilizer plant explosion.

The right way would be to examine each regulation individually, make a full cost/benefit analysis on each one, and then eliminate the ones that don't pass the cost/benefit test. But that would be much more difficult. It requires work, and it requires critical thinking.

If only we had a system in place to do this for us…

Many people don't realize this, but such a system already exists. The United States Government Accountability Office (or GAO, formerly the General Accounting Office, established in 1921) works with various agencies to investigate, to report on, and to make suggestions for eliminating waste and duplications in federal government rules and procedures.

The GAO is an arm of Congress, and as such is part of the legislative branch of government. Perhaps the GAO could be doing a better job in eliminating wasteful regulations. Perhaps Congress could clarify the mission of the GAO in order to put more emphasis on the regulatory aspect of its work. The point is that we have a system in place. We do not need to tear down fences without knowing why they were put up in the first place.

"In the matter of reforming things, as distinct from deforming them, there is one plain and simple principle; a principle which will probably be called a paradox.

There exists in such a case a certain institution or law; let us say, for the sake of simplicity, a fence or gate erected across a road. The more modern type of reformer goes gaily up to it and says, "I don't see the use of this; let us clear it away." To which the more intelligent type of reformer will do well to answer: "If you don't see the use of it, I certainly won't let you clear it away. Go away and think. Then, when you can come back and tell me that you do see the use of it, I may allow you to destroy it.

"This paradox rests on the most elementary common sense. The gate or fence did not grow there. It was not set up by somnambulists who built it in their sleep. It is highly improbable that it was put there by escaped lunatics who were for some reason loose in the street. Some person had some reason for thinking it would be a good thing for somebody. And until we know what the reason was, we really cannot judge whether the reason was reasonable. It is extremely probable that we have overlooked some whole aspect of the question, if something set up by human beings like ourselves seems to be entirely meaningless and mysterious. There are reformers who get over this difficulty by assuming that all their fathers were fools; but if that be so, we can only say that folly appears to be a hereditary disease. But the truth is that nobody has any business to destroy a social institution until he has really seen it as a historical institution. If he knows how it arose, and what purposes it was supposed to serve, he may really be able to say that they were bad purposes, or that they have since become bad purposes, or that they are purposes which are no longer served. But if he simply stares at the thing as a senseless monstrosity that has somehow sprung up in his path, it is he and not the traditionalist who is suffering from an illusion." ~ G.K. Chesterton, "The Thing" (1929)

Section 6: Taxes

Investments and Tax Law

(Originally published August 13, 2014 for The Blue Route Blog)

Economists make a distinction between physical investments and financial investments for a good reason.

Physical investments are direct inputs into businesses such as plant and equipment, plus anything that provides inventory such as raw materials and labor. When economists talk about investments, and the context doesn't indicate otherwise, they are talking about physical investments. They are not talking about the source of the funds behind these physical investments.

When people want to make money off of their accumulated wealth through investments, they tend to be thinking about financial investments. Financial investments are purely financial instruments that are generally categorized as equity (ownership rights, or shares of stock) and debt (loans and bonds). Holders of financial investments tend to think of their stocks and bonds as being their investments, not the physical assets that these financial instruments might or might not be used to purchase in the operations of businesses.

Why is this distinction important? Physical investments go directly into the economy and are used to create economic growth in the overall economy. Financial investments come in many different forms, many of which do not involve direct investment in the economy. Some even take wealth out of the economy, such as overseas bank accounts and the export of jobs instead of goods produced domestically. Some financial investments are mere speculations and do nothing to produce anything in the economy. Often, when investments are purely financial in nature with no corresponding physical investment, the only things that they create are financial bubbles. We all know what happens when these bubbles burst – everybody pays.

Yet tax laws give preferential treatment to financial investments without taking this distinction into consideration. Investment income tends to be taxed at a lower rate than income earned from wages on a job. Tax laws are more generous towards investment income under the theory that investments help to grow the economy. This makes little sense as long as the same tax laws do not make a distinction between investments that actually go towards economic production, investments that create financial bubbles, and investments that take wealth out of the economy. As it currently stands, tax laws actually give investors an incentive to undermine the economy.

Although wages are generally taxed at a higher rate than financial investments, a much higher percentage of wage income gets put back into the economy than investment income. It is time for tax laws to be changed in order to reward activities that benefit the economy and dissuade people from undermining the economy.

There Are No Fair Taxes

(Originally published February 26, 2015 for The Blue Route Blog)

If you are using the concept of fairness as a basis for arguing the pros and cons of any specific type of tax, your arguments are more rhetorical than rational. There are no fair taxes.

All types of taxes are inherently unfair

The issue being discussed here is the distribution of the tax burden. The issue of the total amount of taxes collected by the government is a completely separate issue. Try not to get taken in by any rhetoric which confuses these two issues. For the purpose of this discussion, you can think of a fixed level of government revenue from taxes. When somebody's taxes go down, then somebody else's taxes go up. If we decrease the tax burden for one group of people, then some other group(s) will see an increase in their tax burden.

Taxes can be progressive, regressive, or proportional

Progressive taxes place more of the tax burden on those with a higher ability to pay (higher income or higher wealth). People who get taxed more due to progressive taxes claim that it is unfair that they have to pay a higher percentage to the government than others. It's their money; they earned it.

Regressive taxes place more of the tax burden on those with less ability to pay. People who get taxed more due to regressive taxes claim that it is unfair that they have to pay a higher percentage to the government than others. It's their money, too; and they need it to survive.

Proportional taxes take the same percentage from everybody regardless of ability to pay. But proportional taxes are actually regressive taxes in the sense that they place more of the tax burden on those with less ability to pay. Proportional taxes are regressive taxes masquerading as "equitable" taxes. Flat taxes are proportional taxes which are regressive. Despite the rhetoric, flat taxes are not "fair" taxes. Even if flat tax rates require a minimum income requirement before taxes are paid, those just above the minimum will have a higher tax burden than those far above the minimum.

Even progressive taxes can be viewed as being regressive, if the degree of progression in tax rates is less than the percentage change in the ability to pay.

If all types of taxes are unfair, which type should be used?

*

"Taxes are the price we pay for a civilized society."
~Attributed to Oliver Wendell Holmes in a 1904 speech

*

The answer depends on what kind of society we wish to have. Even if we could reach a consensus on which taxes are more "fair" than others (and we can't), then what happens if we create negative consequences in our society for no other reason than a sense of fairness in our methods? For example, if we as a society have the ability to prevent people from starving to death, should we let them starve if it means that saving them would be "unfair" to those with the ability to pay a little more in taxes? Should we take money out of the hands of those who need that money to survive and would spend it – thus increasing consumer demand and jobs – simply because it would be "unfair" to increase the tax burden on those who have a higher ability to pay? What if our adherence to "fairness" might cause a recession or worse? On the other hand, should we place such a high tax burden on those with a higher ability to pay that we end up taking away incentives for work, entrepreneurship, and investment?

Simply put, no single type of tax is consistent with a stable economy, economic growth, economic freedom, advances in technology, increases in the standard of living, and the opportunity for everybody to live the "American Dream". If we depend too much on one type of tax, placing most of the burden on the same groups of people, then people who feel oppressed by the "system" will eventually rise up, putting at risk the survival of our system of government.

As a result of these considerations, Americans are subject to a mixture of various types of taxes, not just ones which place most of the tax burden on the same groups of people. Everybody pays taxes. The pain of the tax bite is spread around. This doesn't mean that we have an optimal distribution of the tax burden. Far from it – we can always do better. It just means that we don't have to rely on a single type of tax.

When we add all of these types of taxes together, the result is that taxes in the United States tend to be progressive, but perhaps not as progressive as some people may think.

"The necessaries of life occasion the great expense of the poor. They find it difficult to get food, and the greater part of their little revenue is spent in getting it. The luxuries and vanities of life occasion the principal expense of the rich, and a magnificent house embellishes and sets off to the best advantage all the other luxuries and vanities which they possess. A tax upon house-rents, therefore, would in general fall heaviest upon the rich; and in this sort of inequality there would not, perhaps, be anything very unreasonable. It is not very unreasonable that the rich should contribute to the public expense, not only in proportion to their revenue, but something more than in that proportion." ~Adam Smith, The Wealth of Nations, Book 5, Chapter II, Part II, Article I, p. 911.

*

Some additional points to consider:

Stated (or nominal) tax rates and marginal tax rates are NOT the same thing as effective tax rates. The effective rate is the rate that is actually paid. The rhetoric may say that corporations pay 35% in federal taxes, but NO corporation pays that much. Some very profitable corporations have an effective tax rate that is less than zero. For all types of progressive taxes, the effective rate is always lower than the marginal rate.

The same income is subject to various types of taxes. It makes little sense to single out one type of tax, and then criticize it because it represents "double taxation". They all do.

Each type of tax represents a decrease in the ability for someone to engage in certain types of "socially desirable" economic activities. It makes little sense to single out one type of tax, and then criticize it for its potentially negative consequences, unless the consequences of alternative types of taxes are also taken into consideration.

When taxes decrease the ability to engage in certain types of activities, they provide incentives for other types of activities. People and businesses often look for something to use their money on which will decrease their tax bills – invest profits in things which can be written off as pre-tax expenses, for example.

For this analysis, I treated the amount of government revenue from taxes as a separate issue – which it is – in order to focus on the distribution of taxes rather than the total amount of taxes. The truth is that different types of taxes actually CREATE changes in total government revenue.

For example, lower tax rates on corporations will allow corporations to keep more of their revenue, and this additional money will be used, in the aggregate, for a variety of things. Only a percentage of it will be used for new jobs or higher wages for average workers. Lower tax rates on rich individuals will result in additional disposable income which will be used, in the aggregate, for a number of things, only some of which will involve benefits for the overall economy. Lower tax rates for lower-income individuals will result in additional disposable income which largely will be used, in the aggregate, for things which WILL benefit the overall economy. This is because lower-income people are much more likely to spend their disposable income in the domestic economy, increasing demand.

It makes little sense to advocate for lower tax rates for corporations and rich individuals on the basis that they will invest a portion of the extra cash in the economy, unless you also take into consideration that the alternative – lower taxes on low-income individuals – will result in a higher percentage of the money going back into the economy. This can create a broader tax base, increasing government revenue while decreasing government expenditures on social programs.

Talking about "fairness" can confuse the issue.

Section 7: Unemployment

What is the Real Unemployment Rate?

(Originally published August 4, 2014 for The Blue Route Blog)

25%? Much Higher than 25%? If you think the real unemployment rate is even close to being as high as 25%, please read this because the situation isn't anywhere close to being as bad as you think.

We hear a lot about how the "real" unemployment rate is much higher than the "official" unemployment rate. These comments are often accompanied by a specific number that is supposed to accurately reflect the "real" unemployment rate. For purposes of understanding the state of the economy, the concept that the official unemployment rate understates reality is valid. However, coming up with a specific number that reflects a "real" unemployment rate is not as simple as it sounds. There are many different equally logical approaches to defining a "real" unemployment rate that would yield different results.

Let's take a look at who is and isn't included in the "official" unemployment statistics. Let's begin with the formula used:

Unemployment rate = number of unemployed persons divided by the total civilian labor force

The unemployment rate is calculated from data provided by a monthly household survey conducted for the Bureau of Labor Statistics (BLS). It is published, along with other employment data, in a monthly news release.

The total civilian labor force is defined by BLS as those persons classified as employed plus those persons classified as unemployed.

Employed persons: Quoting from the BLS Technical Note accompanying the monthly news release:

People are classified as employed if they did any work at all as paid employees during the reference week; worked in their own business, profession, or on their own farm; or worked without pay at least 15 hours in a family business or farm. People are also counted as employed if they were temporarily absent from their jobs because of illness, bad weather, vacation, labor-management disputes, or personal reasons.

Unemployed persons: Again quoting from the BLS Technical Note:

People are classified as unemployed if they meet all of the following criteria: they had no employment during the reference week; they were available for work at that time; and they made specific efforts to find employment sometime during the 4-week period ending with the reference week. Persons laid off from a job and expecting recall need not be looking for work to be counted as unemployed. The unemployment data derived from the household survey in no way depend upon the eligibility for or receipt of unemployment insurance benefits.

For reference and as an example for what follows, the unemployment rate for March 2014 was 6.7%, calculated from approximately 10.5 million unemployed persons divided by a total civilian labor force of a little over 156 million.

People who don't meet the above criteria for either employed persons or unemployed persons are not considered to be part of the labor force, and are excluded from the calculations for the unemployment rate. The reason is that the unemployment rate is designed to measure how many of the people who want jobs are able to get one, taking into consideration that those who are not actively looking for work are not likely to get a job. With this concept in mind, those who are not working, and not actively looking for work, are categorized as not in the labor force. They are not part of the unemployment rate calculation, but that doesn't mean that they are not counted.

The question becomes, if you conclude that many of these people don't have jobs because of economic conditions, and therefore their non-employed status reflects a hidden unemployment, then which ones should be counted in order to arrive at a "real" unemployment rate? The answer may not be as simple as it first appears.

Suppose, for example, that a person meets all of the criteria for being classified as unemployed, except that they have not looked for work in the past 4 weeks. They want to work, they are available for work, they have looked for work in the past, but their current situation indicates that job search at this particular point in time would be futile, so they accept their plight and don't look for work. People in this category are not classified as either employed or unemployed. They are classified as not in the work force, and are part of the hidden unemployed. There is even a name for people in this category: discouraged workers. They are not in the "official" unemployment statistics, but they are counted. In March 2014, their numbers totaled approximately 700,000. This number was reported in the same news release that the official unemployment rate was reported, but didn't make the headlines to the same degree. I would have to assume that most people searching for a "real" unemployment rate would include these people as unemployed. If we want to include them in the March 2014 calculations, then we would add that number to both the total number of unemployed persons and the total civilian labor force. That would give us an unemployment rate of 11.2 million divided by 157 million, or 7.1%. Adding discouraged workers to the official unemployment calculation would raise the unemployment rate from 6.7% to 7.1% for March 2014.

But I see reports of many people claiming that the "real" unemployment rate is much higher than this. There must be other categories that they include in their calculations. What if the person who wants to work, but hasn't looked for work in the past 4 weeks, has quit looking for work for a different reason other than just giving up? What if that person gave up, and then later committed to doing something else, something that would prevent that person from taking a job if one were offered? Suppose, for example, that person enrolled in college and has committed a certain time frame for education, perhaps a semester or an entire degree program? Should that person still be counted as part of the "real" unemployment rate even if he wouldn't take a job if one were offered? What if a person wanted a job, but illness or injury prevented him from looking for employment for an extended period of time? Should that person be in the same statistics? What if a person was forced to take care of a sick family member and couldn't take a job if one were offered, even though that person would prefer to take a paid job? What if a person couldn't look for work due to transportation problems?

Believe it or not, these people are counted in the BLS data. They just are not part of the official unemployment statistic. How many of these people do you think rightly deserve to be part of the "real" unemployment rate? I suppose the answer depends on what point you are trying to make. If you are counting underproduction in the economy, perhaps most or all of them should be counted. If you were trying to make the point that these people would be working if the economy were performing better, then perhaps you would have to count some but not count others. For the sake of argument, let's count all of them. They are lumped together by the BLS in a category called "marginally attached to the labor force". Let's add them all back in and see how that changes the unemployment rate. This category already includes the discouraged workers that we added in above, so we won't double those calculations. We'll go back to the original 6.7% and add in all of the marginally attached persons. That number for March 2014 was a little over 2 million. If we add that number to both the number of unemployed persons and the total labor force, we get an unemployment rate of about 12.5 million divided by about 158 million, or 7.9%. Adding in all of the marginally attached persons to the ranks of the unemployed, even if doing so is somewhat questionable, would raise the unemployment rate from 6.7% to 7.9%. This is a sizeable jump, but the numbers fall well short of some numbers that I see quoted as the "real" unemployment rate.

What about those who work part time? People get counted as employed if they have a job. It doesn't matter if they work part-time or full-time, or if they have more than one job. If they are employed, they simply get counted once as employed. Many of these people want to work full-time, but due to economic conditions they are only offered part-time work. These people are classified as being underemployed; but in the official statistics, they are simply "employed". What would happen if we added them to the ranks of "unemployed" for the purpose of coming up with what we consider to be an accurate "real" unemployment rate? Doing so would probably distort reality, because it would discount all of the production that is already being done by these part time workers. But since they want to work full-time and are only working part-time, let's count them all as unemployed instead of their current classification of employed. We can't count all part time workers in this category, but we can count the ones who would rather work full-time. They are already being counted, and are included in the data released by the BLS alongside the official unemployment rate. The BLS data has them listed as "part-time for economic reasons" and include not only people who could only find part-time work, but people who have been reduced to part-time due to slow business conditions that perhaps are temporary. Let's count them all; that number is approximately 7.4 million people. That's a lot of people, and it will make a huge difference in the unemployment rate. Let's go back to our last adjustment, which counts all of the marginally attached persons, and change 7.4 million from employed to unemployed. That would change our unemployment rate calculation to about 20 million divided by about 158 million, or 12.7%. That is higher than any annual unemployment rate since official records have been kept, beginning shortly after WWII. The unofficial unemployment rate during the Great Depression was more than twice as high.

This brings up an important point about comparing the unemployment rate from one point in time to another point in time. We have used some very questionable calculation adjustments to get from the official rate of 6.7% to a "real" rate of 12.7%. It is not logical to take that adjusted figure, 12.7%, and compare it to an official figure of an earlier point in time. If you make adjustments, rational or questionable, to one point of comparison, then you need to make the same adjustments to the other point of comparison. Otherwise, the comparison makes absolutely no sense. So the reference above about the historical unemployment rates compared to our adjusted rate of 12.7%? That was going beyond the questionable adjustments we made to raise the current rate to 12.7%. That was adding an irrational comparison.

What is the "real" unemployment rate? I don't have an answer. If you want to make the point that it is different from the official unemployment rate, then any number that you come up with must be based on data that is consistent with the point that you are trying to make. We didn't do that in the calculations above, we just added in whatever real numbers we could justify in order to make the unemployment rate look as large as possible. But what kinds of points would we be making that would justify using a real unemployment rate that is higher than the official unemployment rate?

Are we trying to say that the economy has not recovered as much as the official numbers show?

Are we trying to compare today with a specific point in the past, perhaps for political reasons?

Are we trying to say that the economy is operating at far below capacity?

Are we trying to say that there are more people who are hurting for lack of jobs than what the official numbers indicate?

Are we trying to say that too few workers are supporting too many free-loaders?

Perhaps each one of these points would require making different judgments as to which of the types of situations we would be justified in making adjustments for in the calculations. Do we count part-timers as unemployed instead of employed? Which categories of marginally attached individuals should be included, instead of blindly including all of them like we did? Do we really want to count full-time students, temporarily disabled people, stay at home moms, people taking care of sick parents, and the like as unemployed people? Perhaps for some arguments and purposes, but we certainly cannot be justified in doing so across the board.

The only reason anybody even discusses a difference between the official unemployment rate and a "real" unemployment rate is the fact that different people are trying to make different points as to the meaning of the numbers. Certainly, different numbers can be justified for making different points. As long as those insisting on using a certain number or a certain method of calculation clarify which argument they are making, and limit the use of their version of a "real" unemployment rate to that argument only, then there really isn't much of a reason for disagreement. But we do have disagreements which only serve to confuse the issue and help to keep the public misinformed.

And what about using a higher "real" unemployment rate to point out that too few workers are supporting too many others? We have already counted every single marginally attached person; we have reclassified part time workers for economic reasons from employed to unemployed, and we have made these adjustments without regard to appropriateness. We just counted them all. With everything counted, we nearly doubled the unemployment rate from 6.7% to 12.7%. Yet I continue to hear people arguing that the "real" unemployment rate is perhaps double that, to over 25%. How can that be, if we already added in everybody that we could to the ranks of the unemployed? There is no rational approach to the data that would justify a "real" unemployment rate as large as nearly 25% as being reasonably close to reality, unless the only point being made is to compare the "makers" to the "takers". The only way you could come up with a number that high is to count a lot of people who are not even marginally attached to the labor force, and call them all unemployed. If you are trying to make that point, be very careful about the conclusions that you make. If you want to make the point that the "real" unemployment rate is significantly higher than what we calculated here, then you will need to point out that you are counting as unemployed: significant numbers of children, disabled people, retired people, full-time students, caretakers, homemakers, and/or people who live in households that already have breadwinners to support them.

What Everybody Should Know about Unemployment and the Unemployment Rate

(Originally published June 5, 2015 for The Blue Route Blog's Economics Corner)

It is my observation that when people discuss the unemployment rate, including the validity and importance of the government's "official" rate of unemployment, the discussions generally involve misconceptions as well as unnecessary speculation.

Contrary to some widely held beliefs...

...the government does NOT hide numbers, such as the number of people who have given up looking for work, the number of people who work part-time because they can't get a full-time job, etc.

...there is no single percentage, higher than the "official" unemployment rate, which constitutes a "real" unemployment rate.

...the unemployment rate is NOT based on the number of people who collect unemployment benefits.

...people don't quit being counted simply because their unemployment benefits have run out.

How the Unemployment Rate is Determined

The Bureau of Labor Statistics (BLS), a division of the United States Department of Labor, maintains a vast database of employment statistics. Each month, BLS conducts two statistically significant surveys. One is known as the Household Survey, and the other is known as the Establishment Survey. The unemployment rate is based on data from the Household Survey. The Establishment Survey provides BLS with data regarding the total number of jobs in the economy, as well as the number of jobs in different segments of the economy. On the first or second Friday of each month, the BLS issues a press release entitled "Employment Situation Summary," which includes a summary of statistical results from these two surveys. When news organizations report on the unemployment rate, the number of jobs added to the economy last month, etc., they get their information from this news release. If you want to see the source document, rather than relying on news organizations and others to tell you what is important in the numbers, you can easily look it up for yourself on bls.gov. You might be surprised at the amount of information that is collected and reported in the source document – information in addition to what appears in news headlines. Much of the misinformation being passed around about the unemployment rate is caused by people "assuming" beyond the headlines. The data behind the speculation is readily available and reported along with the numbers in the headlines.

For our purposes, we are concerned with the Household Survey. Each month, BLS commissions a telephone survey of American households. Respondents are asked questions for each household member, such as...

Do you have a job? (If you answer "yes", you are counted as employed)

What is your age? (If you don't have a job but you are under the age of 16, you are not considered part of the labor force)

Is any member of the household institutionalized? (People in prisons, mental institutions, etc. are not part of the labor force)

If you have a job, do you work full-time or part-time? If you work part-time, are you looking for full-time work? (The answers to these questions do not affect the "official" unemployment rate, but they are reported and available to anyone who wonders about them)

If you do not have a job, do you want one? (If you answer "no", then you are not counted in the labor force)

If you do not have a job, but you want one, have you actively looked for work within the past 4 weeks? (If you answer "yes", you are counted as being unemployed; you have to be actively looking for work in order to be considered unemployed; otherwise, you are not considered to be part of the labor force)

If you do not have a job, and you haven't looked for work in the past 4 weeks, have you looked for work at any time in the past 12 months? If so, why did you quit looking? (These people are not counted as part of the labor force, and aren't part of the "official" unemployment rate, but they ARE counted, and BLS keeps track of discouraged workers, etc.)

*

The answers given to these types of questions for the Household Survey form the basis for much of the information in the monthly "Employment Situation Summary." There is no need to speculate on the number of people who have given up looking for work. There is no need to speculate on the number of people who are "underemployed" because they are forced by economic conditions to work part-time. These people are counted, and the numbers are reported along with the "official" unemployment rate.

Why Aren't Discouraged Workers and Underemployed People Counted?

As I mentioned above, they are counted, but they are not included in the "official" unemployment statistics. You might not see these numbers in the news headlines, but they are in the same source document that these news organizations use for their headlines.

These numbers are important for many discussions of unemployment. That's why I encourage people to look at the source. Unfortunately, many people assume the numbers do not exist because they don't see them in the headlines.

What's the Difference Between the "Official" Unemployment Rate and the "Real" Unemployment Rate?

There is no such thing as a single "real" unemployment rate. Different measurements for unemployment, including the "official" measurement, give different pieces of information which serve different purposes. The BLS actually calculates six different unemployment rates – U1 through U6 – for different purposes. The "official" rate is U3. The one which yields the highest unemployment rate is U6.

Different measurements make sense for different purposes. In other words, no single measurement is the "real" one.

Are we trying to say that the economy has not recovered as much as the official numbers show?

Are we trying to compare today with a specific point in the past, perhaps for political reasons?

Are we trying to say that the economy is operating at far below capacity?

Are we trying to say that there are more people who are hurting for lack of jobs than what the official numbers indicate?

Are we trying to say that too few workers are supporting too many free-loaders?

There is no single "real" unemployment rate which would be ideal for a discussion of all of these points.

Don't I Quit Getting Counted as Unemployed if My Benefits Run Out?

Whether or not a person is receiving unemployment benefits is irrelevant to this discussion, other than to point out commonly held misconceptions. The data for the unemployment rate comes from the monthly Household Survey commissioned by the Bureau of Labor Statistics. BLS does not consult any unemployment benefits data, which is maintained on a weekly – not a monthly – basis. Since unemployment benefits have nothing to do with when a person is counted as being unemployed, they have nothing to do with when a person stops being counted. People stop being counted as unemployed when the answers they give on the Household Survey indicate that they no longer meet the definition for being "officially" unemployed.

What Kinds of Policies will Reduce Unemployment?

In order for policies to effectively reduce the unemployment rate, the policies should address the nature of unemployment. Is unemployment high because of a recession? If so, policies designed to deal with the effects of a recession are the proper policies to use. But if unemployment is high because potential workers don't have the skill sets which potential employers are looking for, then policies designed to deal with a skill mismatch are the proper policies to utilize.

There is no one-size-fits-all set of policies for dealing with unemployment. It depends on the category of unemployment that is creating real or perceived problems. A discussion of specific policies for each category is far beyond the scope of this essay, but I want to point out the categories of unemployment which will determine which types of policies to use.

Economists have identified four separate categories of unemployment.

Cyclical unemployment: Unemployment rises when the economy goes into a downturn, such as during a recession. This type of unemployment is called cyclical unemployment, so named because it is related to the business cycle. Economists often use the term "natural rate of unemployment" to indicate the level of unemployment which would exist in the absence of an economic downturn. Cyclical unemployment is in addition to this natural rate of unemployment. It might help to know that "natural rate of unemployment" is sometimes referred to as "full employment." Full employment should not be confused with zero unemployment.

Structural unemployment: This is the type of unemployment that is caused by job-seekers not having the skills necessary to fill open positions. It implies that enough jobs are available in the economy for these job-seekers, but the people who make hiring decisions don't believe that the job-seekers are qualified for the positions that are available. Structural unemployment is often associated with changes in technology. New technology often requires new job skills as jobs utilizing older technology are eliminated. Sometimes business owners complain about a "shortage" of workers with necessary skills. A "shortage" in economics indicates that a price has been set too low. Higher wages in this situation would eliminate any real shortage (and presumably eliminate the complaints – yet those who are complaining are the ones with the power to eliminate the shortage). Structural unemployment is considered to be part of the natural rate of unemployment.

Frictional unemployment: This is the unemployment that arises from the fact that there is always a time gap between the time when a person without a job starts actively looking for a job, and the time when that person finds a job. In a dynamic economy, many people will fall into this category at any point in time, including the time when the unemployment statistics are compiled.

Frictional unemployment is considered to be part of the natural rate of unemployment.

Seasonal unemployment: This is the unemployment caused by the fact that some jobs have busy seasons and slow seasons. During the slow seasons, many workers are laid off, but will be expected to be rehired once the busy season returns. Seasonal unemployment is considered to be part of the natural rate of unemployment.

Structural, frictional, and seasonal unemployment are all considered to be part of the natural rate of unemployment. Some amount of unemployment in these categories is considered to be good for the economy. Unemployment is a necessary part of a growing economy with new technologies, young workers moving into the labor force, and workers being free to test their marketability. It doesn't make sense to consider the "natural rate of unemployment" to be zero. Still, it is possible to develop policies which would decrease the number of unemployed people who fall into these categories. For example: better education, job training, and job-matching technology.

Section 8: Inflation

"Inflation: Not What You Think it is" – page 113

"What Everybody Should Know about Inflation" –
page 118

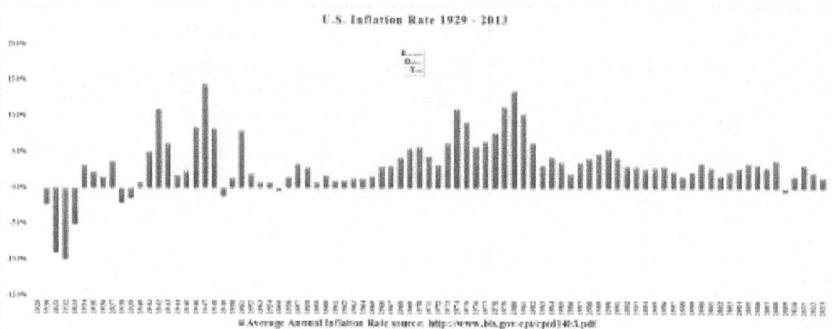

Inflation: Not What You Think it is

(Originally published August 5, 2014 for The Blue Route Blog)

"Inflation: A sustained rise in the average level of prices."

Why do people tend to think of inflation as an evil? Do we have to live with this evil, in a world where we can complain about the problem but in the end we just put up with it, or can we find policies to support which will eliminate this evil? What exactly are the problems in our lives that are caused by inflation?

Well, let's look at some specific problems. With inflation, we lose purchasing power. Our incomes don't go as far as they used to. Our real incomes fall, our wealth is depleted, and more people end up below the poverty line. When our incomes rise due to a cost of living increase, the increase tends to be based on last year's inflation rate. Our expenses, especially living expenses, continue to go up while our incomes are based on old inflation statistics. Our cost of living adjustments (COLAs) are inadequate anyway, never covering our increases in living expenses, even when discounted for a one year delay in receiving the COLAs. An increase in utility expenses by themselves might be more than the entire increase in pay we get to cover inflation. The same thing can be said about many other expenses – food, fuel, and medicine are some of the ones many of us think of first. We might have to choose between these necessities in our monthly budgets.

Meanwhile, businesses and individuals find it harder to receive credit. Banks don't want to lend money if they know that they will be paid back in money that is worth less than it was worth at the time of the loan. Debt will redistribute wealth from creditors (banks, bond investors, etc.) to debtors (borrowers, bond sellers including the government, etc.) due solely to the existence of inflation. Business costs increase, access to funds to invest in business decreases, and as a result businesses lay off more employees. Long term contracts involving payment become riskier than short term agreements, creating a redistribution of resources.

Did I come up with a good description of the evils of inflation? I did not intend to make a comprehensive list of all of the problems associated with inflation, and perhaps you can come up with more. Perhaps you can make a better list than I did. But did I at least do a decent job of summarizing and highlighting the main problems we face with inflation?

If you say yes, then take another look. None of the problems I listed above are examples of inflation. They are things that we always associate with inflation, but they are not examples of inflation. In order to understand this point, go back to the definition of inflation:

Inflation: A sustained rise in the average level of prices.

Prices in this definition include wage rates. Wage rates are prices paid by someone to someone else. Wages are costs as well as income. Interest rates are also prices. Interest is the cost of credit. In the economy, different prices change by different amounts, at different times, and not always in the same direction. Inflation occurs when the average of all of these prices rises. Inflation does not occur simply because one price rises, or because some prices rise. Inflation only occurs when the average of all prices rise. The inflation rate is the rate by which this average price level changes, not the rate by which individual prices change. A one-time rise in prices is not inflation either; the rise must be sustained over time.

So what problems are created by a sustained rise in the average level of prices? None of the problems that I listed, as real as all of them are, falls into this category. Inflation means that over time, people have to get used to big numbers that mean the same thing that small numbers used to mean. Inflation means more time and expense associated with the process of changing prices. – But the bigger problems that I listed above? Inflation does not cause those problems.

None of those problems would exist if all prices moved together at the same time, in the same direction, at the same rate. The inflation rate could be exactly the same, but the problems would not exist. As long as every price change is equal to the average price change, these problems do not exist.

Think about that: the inflation rate could be exactly the same, but the problems would not exist. The definition of inflation depends on the average price change. According to this definition, inflation does not cause these problems. The problems are all caused by individual price variances from the average.

What difference does this truth make? Am I not just parsing words by emphasizing the definition and not the reality of inflation? Are not all of these problems at least side effects of inflation, with the same underlying cause?

It makes a huge difference when it comes to policy decisions. If the policy focus is on the average level of prices, and not on the variances from this average, then the problems listed above will not get solved and more problems might be created as unintended consequences. If the policy focus is on the individual variances, then the problems can be addressed directly.

For example, many senior citizens have their standards of living eroded because of increases in the costs of prescription medication and food items. Policy decisions designed to lower the rate of inflation will do nothing to fix this problem. The source of the problem is the formula and timing of the cost of living adjustments (COLAs) relative to the specific price changes that seniors on fixed incomes tend to be affected by.

In the meantime, a policy of lowering the inflation rate could have unintended consequences on the economy. Remember that the inflation rate is an average of the rate of change of many different prices in the economy, all of which change at different rates, and sometimes in different directions. When the average is lowered, so are some or all of its various components. More prices go down, and deflation becomes a potential problem. Deflation means that businesses sell their products at a lower price level than the one that existed whenever they purchased raw materials. During periods of deflation, the number of business and farm bankruptcies increases. Real interest rates become higher than nominal rates. Unused production capacity, including unemployment, tends to be higher whenever inflation is very low or negative.

On the other hand, if politicians saw the problem faced by a senior citizen on a fixed income for what it really is, then the problem could be addressed at its source. The Social Security income of a senior citizen is indexed by inflation. But the formula that is used does not reflect the spending patterns and necessities of typical seniors. Using several different inflation indexes that are designed for specific purposes, including one for senior citizens living on Social Security, would be one way to address this particular problem. Another would be to directly address the specific price increases faced by senior citizens – for example, policies designed to fight the soaring cost increases for prescription medication.

The problems listed at the beginning of this essay can be dealt with more successfully with a focus on the specific problems than they can be with a focus on the overall rate of inflation. By the way, the problem with credit relationships redistributing wealth solely because of inflation does not really exist, at least not in the way I worded the problem. Wealth gets redistributed when actual inflation varies from expected inflation, and the redistribution can work either way, depending on which direction the actual results vary from the forecasts. This should not be confused with the fact that credit relationships can and do redistribute wealth in ways that are completely unrelated to inflation.

Policies designed to work on the overall inflation rate make sense only when the specific problems being targeted are problems associated with that overall rate. This includes fighting deflation, but it also includes fighting hyperinflation. Under current conditions and policies, deflation has been at times a real problem and currently is a bigger potential problem. We have never experienced hyperinflation in the United States. Hyperinflation would require conditions much different from the ones we face today. Many times throughout American history, we have been subjected to dire warnings about impending hyperinflation that has never materialized.

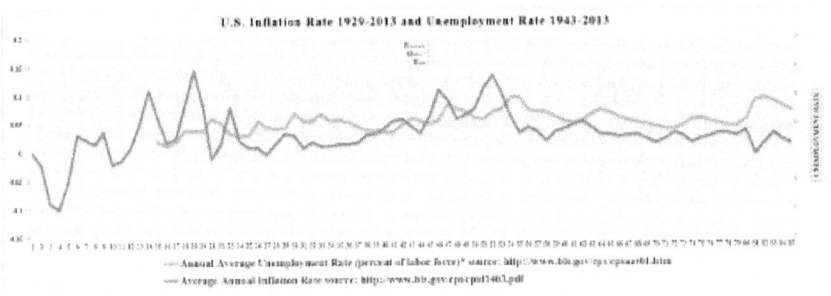

U.S. Inflation Rate 1929-2013 and Unemployment Rate 1943-2013

——Annual Average Unemployment Rate (percent of labor force)* source: http://www.bls.gov/cps/cpsaat01.htm

——Average Annual Inflation Rate source: http://www.bls.gov/cpi/cpiai.pdf

What Everybody Should Know about Inflation

(Originally published May 20, 2015 for The Blue Route Blog's Economics Corner)

Inflation is one of the most widely commented-on yet most widely misunderstood topics on the economy. Everybody seems to have a viewpoint. Yet many of the views are based on misconceptions. Everybody who desires to be an informed voter should learn to distinguish between basic truths and well-meaning but misguided thoughts regarding inflation.

For starters, look at each of the following statements. If you agree with any of them, then you should read this essay to the end. Each of these statements is FALSE.

"Our purchasing power keeps going down because prices keep going up. To fix this problem, we need policies designed to cut the rate of inflation."

"People on fixed incomes increasingly are forced to live in poverty because inflation keeps eating into their incomes. To fix this problem, we need policies designed to cut the rate of inflation."

"Inflation is bad. The economy works best for everybody if the rate of inflation is zero."

"Inflation is always the result of too much money chasing a fixed quantity of goods."

"Inflation is the biggest threat to our economic well-being. We need to cut the rate of inflation at all costs, or we will end up being destroyed by hyperinflation."

"Gasoline prices are not counted in the government's inflation index. If they were, Social Security benefits would be higher."

Each of the above statements is false. If you agree with any of them, then I hope I got your attention. All of these statements are well-intentioned. Most of them begin with an obvious truth, but end up with false assumptions about the kinds of policies needed to address the obviously true problems. All of these statements rely on a misconception of the nature of inflation. As a result of the misconception, all of these statements suggest a misguided policy – a policy which either doesn't address the source of the problem, or will create unintended consequences which are worse than the current problem (or both).

In order to understand the widespread misconceptions about inflation, we need to start with a definition of inflation.

Inflation: A sustained rise in the average level of prices

Hopefully, you would agree that this definition is fairly straightforward. With inflation, a given face-value of currency will provide less purchasing power over time. When we look at it from the point of view of declining purchasing power, we can come up with an alternative way of stating a definition for inflation.

Inflation: A sustained decline in the value of the currency

Again, this definition is fairly straightforward. You might notice that either way of stating a definition of inflation is consistent with the "obvious truths" in some of the above false statements. It is true that purchasing power decreases when the same amount of money can buy fewer things. It is true that a fixed income doesn't go as far when the value of the currency decreases. But if you take a closer look at the definition, you should be able to see that the suggested "solution" of decreasing the rate of inflation doesn't actually deal with the problems listed.

The rate of inflation depends on changes in the average level of prices. One price change doesn't equal the rate of inflation.

The average of all price changes equals the rate of inflation.

If every individual price in the economy changed at exactly the same rate as the average, regardless of how high or low that average happens to be, then none of the problems listed above would exist. Suppose, for example, that the rate of inflation is 5%. This means that the average of all price changes in the economy is a 5% increase per year. If every price increased by 5% at the same time, then the purchasing power of our incomes would stay the same. You have to understand that wages for one is a cost to someone else. Wages are factored into the costs of other items. Wages are prices. As long as every price change is identical, wages would also adjust by the same amount. As long as a cost of living adjustment (COLA) for people on fixed incomes keeps up, these people will not have their purchasing power decrease. Yes, the purchasing power for a fixed quantity of currency will decrease. But this will be offset by incomes increasing by an equivalent amount of currency.

The rate of inflation, then, doesn't cause any of the problems listed. Yet we know that some of these problems do exist. We know that purchasing power decreases. How can this be true, if inflation doesn't create these problems?

Inflation DOES cause these problems. But the RATE of inflation does NOT.

That is the key to understanding policy implications. The truth is that all price changes do not equal the average. Some price changes are higher than the average, and some price changes are lower than the average. Some prices go up at the same time that other prices go down. These variances from the average affect different individuals and different classes of individuals in different ways. If all price changes equaled the average, then these problems do not exist. But when you have variances from the exact same average price change, these problems exist.

Problems typically associated with inflation, including loss of purchasing power, are not problems that can be fixed through policies designed to change the rate of inflation. The rate of inflation has nothing to do with the problems. If we want to deal with these problems effectively, we need to focus on policies which deal with undesirable consequences of variances from the average rate of inflation. For example, if senior citizens on a fixed income are losing purchasing power because the COLA used for determining benefits isn't keeping up with the actual expenses that seniors tend to have, policy focus should be on changing the COLA formula, not on trying to lower the overall rate of inflation in the economy.

But wouldn't the problems go away if prices never changed and the inflation rate was zero?

Whoa there! We could have a zero rate of inflation, with no variances from the average creating these problems; at least in theory. Getting there would require a command economy – an economy in which the government makes every price and production decision. The government could simply freeze all prices. If we were advocating for such an economy – and some people do – then we wouldn't even need to discuss which types of policies would be effective in eliminating the problems associated with inflation. However, if you believe in the benefits of a market-based economy, or even one that is partially based on market forces, then you don't want to go there. A free-market economy requires prices to be able to adjust freely. All of the benefits claimed by advocates of a market-based economy – reallocation of resources to improve efficiency, economic growth, technological advances, consumer choices, upward mobility, fair prices due to competition, elimination of shortages and surpluses, etc. – require that prices be allowed to adjust freely. If we fixed prices in order to eliminate inflation, these benefits wouldn't exist – even in theory.

But still, isn't lower inflation always better than higher inflation?

One way to visualize the fallacy of this argument is to look at the stock listings in the business section of the newspaper. On a typical day, a stock index might go up or down by 1%, more or less. The newspaper will report the amount of change for the index, and that change (points or percentage) is what the headlines will focus on. But if you look at all of the individual listings, you won't see the same percentage change for each item. You will see some upticks and some downticks. Some changes will be relatively large, and some prices won't change at all. The stock index average might be higher than the previous day, or it might be lower. In the long run, stock prices go up. You can't really see the long run trend by looking at the upticks and downticks on a given day. But you can see that for a typical day, some stock prices go up, and some go down, regardless of which direction the average moves. Individual price changes for goods and services in the economy act in a similar fashion. At any point in time, some prices are going up and some are going down. There are upticks and downticks, so to speak. On the average, prices go up in the long run. It is this long run trend in average price changes, not any individual price change, which defines the rate of inflation.

When the rate of inflation increases, then that means either the number of upticks increased relative to the number of downticks, or that the deviation from the average changed. When the rate of inflation decreases, then either the number of downticks increased relative to the number of upticks, or the deviation from the average changed. Neither scenario, by itself, is necessarily better or worse than the other. "Good" or "bad" depends on other factors. Economic growth can be associated with upward pressure on prices. Economic growth means that more resources are being utilized for production purposes. Whenever additional resources are required, average costs go up. For example, if a business needs more man-hours of labor in order to meet a higher demand for its product, then it will either have to pay more for overtime, or bid up labor costs in order to compete with other businesses for available labor. The labor market becomes a seller's market.

On the other hand, price decreases are associated with slower economic growth, or even economic contraction. Resources are idled. Labor is laid off. The labor market becomes a buyer's market.

With lower inflation, economic growth tends to be lower, unemployment tends to be higher, and wages tend to be lower. In fact, the policies used by the Fed when it attempts to lower the rate of inflation are policies specifically designed to lower wages and increase unemployment. Monetary policy by the Fed acts on a trade-off between inflation and unemployment. With higher inflation, the opposite tends to be true. It's all about the reality of price variances from the average and the economic factors which put pressure on prices to either go up or go down.

But aren't high inflation and hyperinflation real problems in the economy?

Yes, high inflation creates real problems. Hyperinflation creates political revolution. But in today's economic and political climate, the chances that policy-makers will go along with a "the sky is falling" mentality of those spreading misinformation about inflation is a bigger danger than the chance that we will experience high inflation any time soon. Economists tend to agree that reaching potential economic growth is consistent with an inflation rate of around 3% to 5%.

When the inflation rate is close to zero, there is more danger of deflation than high inflation. Deflation means that small business and family farm bankruptcies increase because debt obligations are harder to meet when the prices of the goods they sell are going down. Think in terms of the visual comparison to stock market tables – deflation means that there are more downticks, or larger downticks, than upticks.

When the inflation rate is above the rate consistent with potential economic growth, the economy is overheating. Since growth requires the use of more resources, an overheated economy is one where the additional cost associated with using more resources outweighs the additional output resulting from the use of these resources.

Despite the rhetoric from many people, the only way that the United States could fall into a state of hyperinflation would be if the entire political system disintegrated into a state of all-out civil war. Too much is now known about the causes of hyperinflation – and there are too many safeguards in place to prevent such an outcome – that it would take the entire collapse of the political and social system BEFORE hyperinflation would even be possible. In that case, the collapse of the political system along with the advent of civil war – and not some economic policy – would be the cause of the problem.

Hyperinflation is associated with an inflation rate of 50% per month, or higher. The United States has never threatened to approach inflation numbers in that range. The last time we had an inflation rate as high as 10% per year was 1981. Most historical instances of double digit inflation in the United States have been associated with the supply shock of the Arab Oil Embargo of the

1970s. The last time inflation inched above 5% for an entire year was 1990.

Is inflation always caused by "too much money chasing too few goods"?

"Inflation is always a monetary phenomenon" is a common belief. People hear it over and over, assume it must be true, and repeat it. The implication is that the rate of inflation increases proportionally whenever more money is put into circulation, and that the way to eliminate inflation is to hold the money supply steady. Sometimes this claim is accompanied by a mathematical equation purporting to prove that this must be true.

Besides the most obvious example of stagflation – a situation unrelated to the money supply – there isn't much in the historical data to support this claim (not counting the rare special cases of hyperinflation in other countries). Such a claim ignores the processes involving supply and demand of goods and services which put upward and downward pressures on prices as production increases and decreases.

Should gasoline prices be included in the price index?

When gas prices go up, they often go up dramatically, and people whose incomes are indexed to inflation definitely have their purchasing power decreased.

However, gasoline prices are extremely volatile. They go up quickly, but they also go down quickly. The long-run trend of gas prices is roughly the same as the long run trend of prices in general. If gasoline prices were included in the price indexes used for making policy decisions, including the benefits for people on fixed incomes, then economic policy itself would be volatile. People on fixed incomes would see benefits go up, but they would also see benefits go down. Including gasoline prices in policy decisions would create unstable policy.

But there are other ways to "fix" price indexing that seem to make sense. Currently, Social Security benefits are indexed to something called CPI-W. This index is an estimation of changes in purchasing power based on the spending patterns of "typical" urban wage earners and clerical workers. But people who receive Social Security benefits do not have the same spending patterns as these "typical" workers. "Urban wage earners and clerical workers" as a group spend more money on electronics and other decreasing-cost items. They are more likely to have discretionary income, which makes it easier to substitute low-cost items for high-cost items when prices change. On the other hand, senior citizens who receive Social Security benefits spend more of their money on increasing-cost items such as prescription medication. As a group, they spend a larger share of their incomes on necessities for which fewer low-cost substitutes exist. One way to eliminate the effects of inflation on the purchasing power of senior citizens is to index Social Security benefits to items that senior citizens tend to spend their money on. Another way would be to develop policies which deal directly with the increasing costs of prescription medication.

Is inflation a self-fulfilling prophecy?

There can be a herd-mentality factor in the rate of inflation. If customers expect prices to go up, they might rush to buy, causing prices to go up due to an increase in demand. If businesses expect costs to go up, they might decrease long-term investments, causing prices to go up due to a decrease in supply.

Section 9: The Minimum Wage

"Raising the Minimum Wage does not Kill Jobs" –

**"Debunking Arguments against a Minimum Wage
Increase"** –

Raising the Minimum Wage does not Kill Jobs

(Originally published August 4, 2014 for The Blue Route Blog)

People who claim that raising the minimum wage will cause job losses never cite the actual historical record, because history shows the opposite to be true. With very few exceptions, the economy has grown and the number of jobs has increased following each increase in the minimum wage. There is absolutely no statistical record to justify a claim that a minimum wage increase will cause job losses.

They can't cite the actual record, so instead they quote conclusions from economic theory. Many times, they even use haughty language to demean those who disagree with them, such as "people in favor of raising the minimum wage don't understand basic Econ 101". In reality, those who say such things are the ones who miss the point of what these theories taught in Econ 101 are actually saying.

What about the assumptions behind the theory? How do they affect the outcome when real-world circumstances, without the isolating assumptions, are taken into consideration? What effect does an increase in the minimum wage have on the demand and supply in both the product markets and the labor markets? How do the demand and supply curves shift as a result? What effect does the fact that the demand for labor is derived from the demand for products and services have on the theoretical conclusions? What is the elasticity of supply, and what is the elasticity of demand in the various markets that are affected by an increase of the minimum wage? How does this change the outcome? How does the fact that the economy does not have one labor market with every potential worker being eligible for the labor supply, but instead consists of many different labor markets for different jobs in different product markets, different skill levels, different geographical locations, etc. affect the conclusions of the theory? How does the fact that the world doesn't consist of all (or any) markets that are perfectly-competitive, but instead consists almost entirely of markets which can best be described as oligopoly or monopoly, affect the conclusions of the theory? What about the "before" situation in the theory? Can it really represent free-market equilibrium when free markets have never existed outside the theoretical world? If the beginning point is a point of labor exploitation and one-sided policies that give corporations more market power than workers and consumers have, how can the conclusions really have any "free market" meaning at all? What is the cumulative effect of previous policies on this "equilibrium"?

These are all valid points that together explain why the real-world results are so far from the theoretical conclusions. They are all points taught in Econ 101 that apparently are forgotten by those who cite theoretical conclusions or superior knowledge of Econ 101 to argue against raising the minimum wage.

Debunking Arguments against a Minimum Wage Increase

(Originally published October 7, 2014 for The Blue Route Blog)

Arguments against an increase in the minimum wage tend to be along the lines of one or more of the following:

"Businesses will lay off workers, hurting the same people that the minimum wage is supposed to help." I call this argument the Unemployment Argument.

"Businesses will simply pass along the cost increase to their customers in the form of higher prices, and workers won't be any better off than before due to inflation caused by the minimum wage increase." I call this argument the Inflation Argument.

"The cost increase will force businesses to cut production, and the economy will tank." I call this argument the Trickle-down Argument.

Each of these arguments could also be called the Econ 101 argument. This is because such arguments often use language such as "If you knew basic economics, you would know this is true". Sometimes the language is a little stronger, implying that "I oppose an increase in the minimum wage because I understand economics. If you support an increase in the minimum wage, it proves that you don't understand basic economics. Therefore, your viewpoint is invalid".

When somebody uses these kinds of arguments, you can respond by asking them to read this essay. Such arguments are being made by people who don't understand basic economics as well as they think they do.

First of all, you need to know where these arguments are coming from. What exactly do people mean when they invoke an Econ 101 argument?

The Econ 101 Argument

An Econ 101 argument has its basis in a graph such as this one:

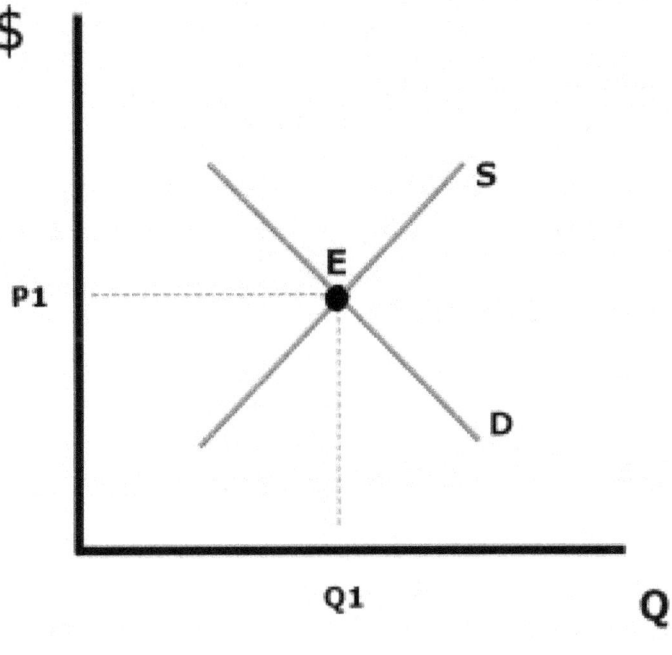

Figure 1

Figure 1 is a basic supply & demand diagram. It is an example of a visual representation of concepts taught in economics classes. This one is a basic diagram from which more complex concepts and diagrams are based. It plots the relationship between price and quantity in a typical market. The point where the heavy vertical

131

and horizontal lines meet is called the origin. The vertical line labeled $ represents price. The farther you go up the line, away from the origin, the higher the price. The horizontal line labeled Q represents quantity. The farther you go out away from the origin, the higher the quantity.

Within the heavy lines, in the plot area, are two more lines, labeled S and D. The line labeled S is the supply curve. It is a visual representation of the Law of Supply, which states that as the price increases, the quantity that suppliers are willing to supply increases as well; and as the price decreases, the quantity that suppliers are willing to supply decreases. In other words, there is a positive relationship between price and the quantity supplied – the quantity changes in the same direction that price changes. Businesses are willing and able to sell more if they can get a higher price. This gives the supply curve an upward slope.

The line labeled D is the demand curve. It is a visual representation of the Law of Demand, which states that as the price increases, the quantity that buyers are willing to buy decreases; and as the price decreases, the quantity that buyers are willing to buy increases. In other words, there is a negative relationship between price and the quantity demanded – the quantity changes in the opposite direction of a price change. Consumers are willing and able to buy more when the price is lower. This gives the demand curve a downward slope.

The benefits of free-market economics, the Invisible Hand, and the resulting efficiency gains all stem from the concepts behind the diagram in Figure 1. Other, more complicated graphs in economics classes are extensions of the concepts behind this one. Since the supply curve (S) slopes upward, and the demand curve (D) slopes downward, the efficient market price and quantity will be the price and quantity where these two curves intersect. In Figure 1, the market price is labeled P1, which is the price at which the supply and demand curves intersect, and the market quantity is labeled

Q1, which is the quantity at which the supply and demand curves intersect. The point of intersection, labeled E in Figure 1, is the market equilibrium point. It is sometimes referred to as the efficiency point, representing the price and quantity deemed most efficient.

This quick overview of a supply and demand diagram is necessary for understanding the Econ 101 arguments against increasing the minimum wage. The diagram in Figure 1 is for a generic market. The labor market is also a market in which the same supply and demand concepts apply. The supply curve in the labor market slopes upward. The demand curve in the labor market slopes downward. The equilibrium, or efficiency, point is where these two curves intersect.

Everything in this diagram is the same in the labor market as it is in a market for widgets. In the labor market, the price is the wage rate. The demand for labor is the quantity of labor (number of workers) that employers wish to hire at each wage rate. The supply of labor is the quantity of labor that workers are willing to supply at each wage rate. In this sense, there is a sort-of role reversal – those who are suppliers in the product and service markets are the demanders of labor.

From here, we can add in the variable of an increase in the minimum wage and see graphically what the Econ 101 arguments are all about.

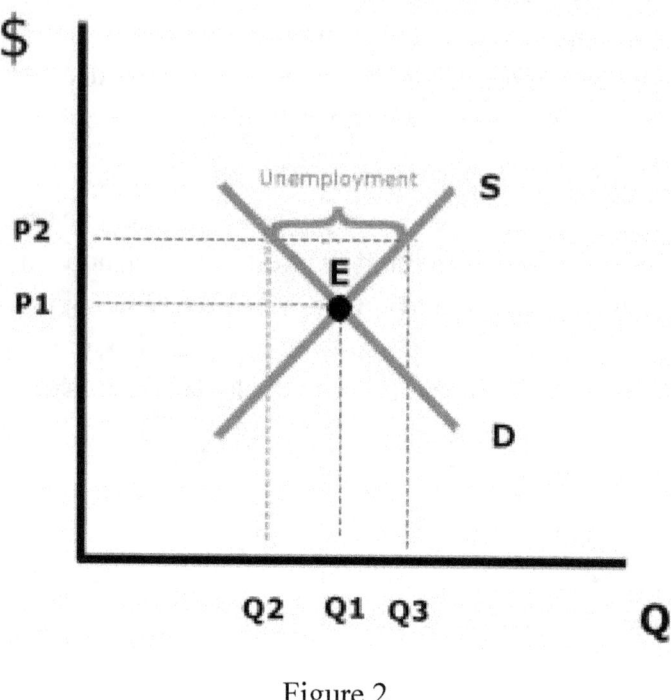

Figure 2

Figure 2 is identical to Figure 1, except that it is specific to a labor market with a minimum wage set above the equilibrium wage. P1 is the prevailing market wage rate, identical to the price labeled "P" in Figure 1. Q1 is the amount of employment in this market if there is no minimum wage set above the prevailing wage. P2 is a minimum wage set above the prevailing wage.

If the wage rate is changed from P1 to P2, look at what happens to employment. Due to the slopes of the supply and demand curves, this new wage rate intersects the demand curve at a lower quantity of labor (labeled Q2) than the equilibrium quantity of labor (labeled Q1); while at the same time, it intersects the supply curve at a higher quantity of labor (labeled Q3) than the equilibrium quantity of labor (Q1).

In other words, employers are willing to hire fewer workers at a higher wage rate, but workers are willing to supply more labor at a higher wage rate. So how many people will get work? It doesn't matter that more people are willing to work if employers are willing to hire fewer workers. You can't get a job if nobody wants to hire you. The lower quantity will prevail, in this case the quantity that is determined by the demand for labor curve.

The amount by which Q2 is lower than Q1 represents the number of jobs that will be lost due to an increase in the minimum wage (you can measure this lost labor in terms of hours worked instead of in terms of jobs, but the message of this generic approach is that people will lose wage income one way or another). The difference between Q2 and Q1 is new unemployment created by the increase in the minimum wage. But since more workers are willing to work at the higher wage, the difference between Q1 and Q3 is also new unemployment. Therefore, unemployment increases by the total amount of (Q3 minus Q2), with (Q1 minus Q2) being the number of people laid off due to the minimum wage, and (Q3 minus Q1) being the number of people formerly not in the labor market who are now looking for work due to the higher wage rate. Unemployment increases by a higher rate than the number of people who are laid off, due to the slopes of the supply & demand curves.

The conclusion reached is that with a minimum wage, fewer people will find work. More people will be unemployed. This only applies if the minimum wage is set above the prevailing market wage, because a minimum wage is a price floor. If a minimum wage is already in effect, and the analysis is about raising it to a higher wage rate, then the higher minimum wage will increase both the number of jobs lost and the unemployment rate.

This is the essence of the Unemployment Argument against an increase in the minimum wage. When someone tells you that an increase in the minimum wage will increase unemployment and hurt those it is supposed to help, because "everybody who understands basic economics knows this", go ahead and ask them to explain what they mean. Perhaps they can't explain it, because they don't understand it themselves and they are only repeating what they have heard. But if they do try to explain it, then their explanation will be a form of the explanation that I just gave here.

What about the other Econ 101 arguments – the Inflation argument and the Trickle-down argument?

These arguments involve more than the labor market. They involve production and the sale of goods and services produced in the economy. They involve the product markets – the market for widgets, so to speak.

You have to understand that the demand for labor is a derived demand. People and businesses don't hire and pay workers because they are in the business of paying workers. They are in the business of earning a profit. Producing and selling widgets is the method they use for earning a profit. But the process of producing and selling widgets involves labor, so these businesses need to hire labor in order to realize their objectives. If they could find a cheaper method for getting the same results, one that would increase profits, they would do so. The demand for labor is derived from the demand for widgets. So we need to look at the market for widgets.

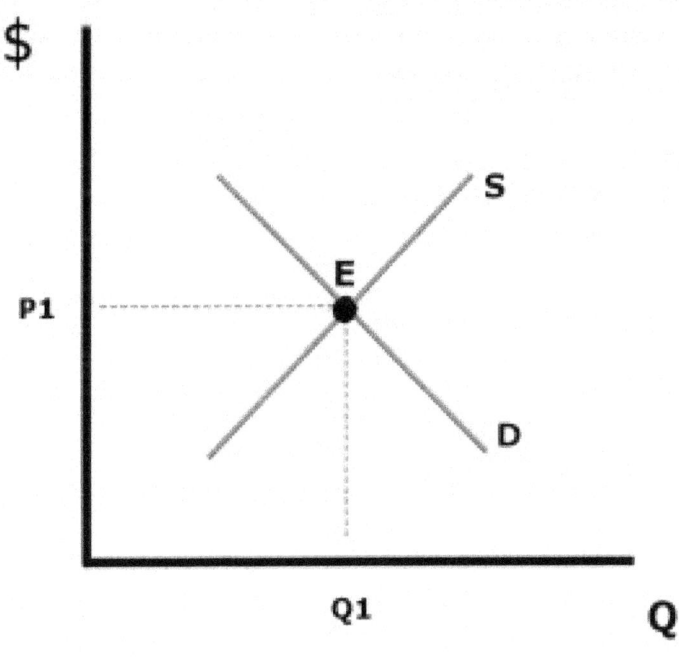

Figure 3

Figure 3 is identical to Figure 1 above. The only difference is that Figure 1 was used as a reference for an analysis of the labor market, and Figure 3 is for a product or service market – the market for widgets in this generic explanation. The same supply & demand properties apply to all kinds of markets, so the same generic graph also applies to all markets. In this example, P1 is the free market price of widgets, and Q1 is the quantity of widgets that will be produced and sold at that price. P1 is considered to be the efficiency price, and Q1 is considered to be the efficiency quantity. This graph shows the widget market in equilibrium.

What happens to the market for widgets when an increase in the minimum wage causes the cost of producing widgets to go up?

One of the factors of supply is the price of resources, and labor is a resource in the market for widgets. When the price of labor

137

increases, the supply of widgets will decrease regardless of the demand for widgets. This means that the widget market moves from the equilibrium situation shown in Figure 3, to a new equilibrium situation as shown by Figure 4.

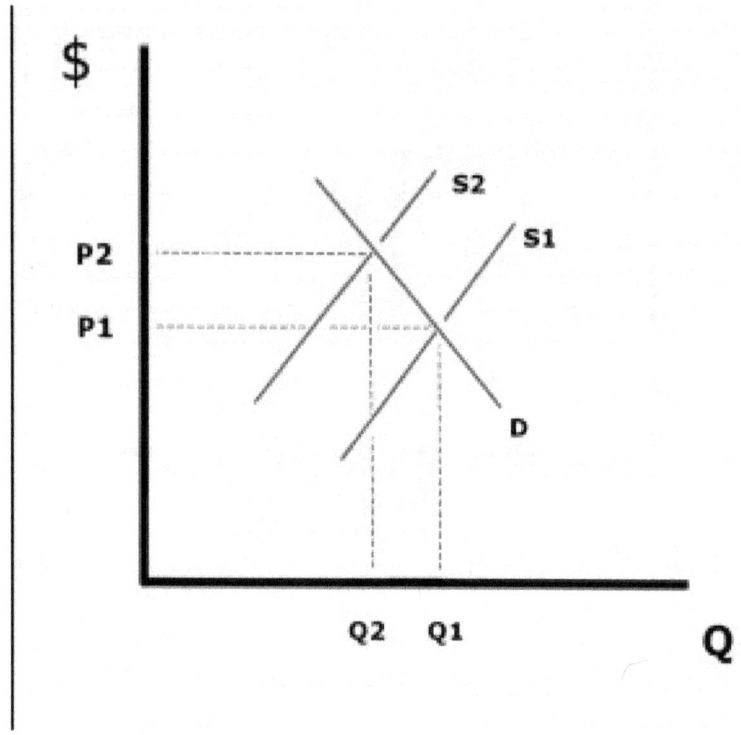

Figure 4

D, S1, P1 and Q1 in Figure 4 represent the same equilibrium situation as D, S, P1, and Q1 in Figure 3. This is the equilibrium in the market for widgets before an increase in the minimum wage goes into effect. But when you introduce an increase in the minimum wage, which involves a decrease in the supply of widgets as explained above, then the supply curve shifts from S1 to S2. P2 becomes the new equilibrium price of widgets, and Q2 becomes the new equilibrium quantity of widgets produced. You will note that P2 is higher than P1 and that Q2 is lower than Q1. In other words, an increase in the minimum wage has caused the price of widgets to increase (the Inflation Argument against an increase in the minimum wage), while at the same time it has caused the production of widgets to decrease (the Trickle-down Argument against an increase in the minimum wage).

These are the Econ 101 arguments against an increase in the minimum wage. Again, when someone mentions Econ 101 as a reason for opposing an increase in the minimum wage, you should ask them what they mean. Ask for a detailed explanation. If they can't tell you, it's probably because they don't know and they are simply repeating what they have heard. But if they do give you an explanation, and do so in a way that sounds like they know what they are talking about, then they will say something along the lines of my explanation above.

You should note that this explanation does involve a higher price in the generic widget market, and therefore higher prices in all markets affected by an increase in the minimum wage. But it does NOT support the claim that "businesses will simply raise their prices to cover the cost increase". The price does go up, but not by the full amount of the increase in cost. If you look at Figure 4, you will see that the difference between S1 and S2 is larger than the difference between P1 and P2. This is due to basic supply & demand principles involving the downward slope of the demand curve. A price increase is definitely involved, but not for the full amount of the cost increase.

Other than that minor detail, the Econ 101 Argument involves conclusions based on the above analysis of concepts taught in a basic economics course.

If you understand everything that I have said so far, but at the same time you have never taken an actual economics course, then congratulations! You now have a basic working knowledge of some of the most important principles of microeconomics. Not nearly all of the important principles that you would find in an Econ 101 course, but at least the ones that are being used to invoke an Econ 101 argument against an increase in the minimum wage.

Debunking the Econ 101 Argument

Unfortunately for those who claim superior knowledge of basic economics when they invoke an Econ 101 argument against an increase in the minimum wage, their conclusions have two fatal flaws.

1. The historical record does not support their claims.

2. Their conclusions are based on a faulty understanding of the concepts that they claim to understand better than anybody who supports an increase in the minimum wage.

The Historical Record

An increase in the minimum wage isn't a theoretical concept. It is something that has been done many times before, and there is a fairly extensive historical record of the results. Why would you listen to someone who tells you what will happen, according to some graphs in an economics course, when you can go to the actual record and see what has happened in the real world? After all, we are talking about real-world policies here. We are concerned about real-world results.

Some people like to butt in when the discussion turns towards real-world results of a particular policy change, and say something along the lines of "but there were other things going on in the economy that led to those results; this policy didn't do it". This is an argument people use whenever they cannot accept the idea that their ideology is wrong. Such an argument can indeed be valid in specific situations, but not in the case of the results of a minimum wage increase. The historic record is too extensive.

Since the introduction of a minimum wage in the United States, the minimum wage has been increased 21 times – spread out over the years between 1939 and 2009. The minimum wage increases have come at varying stages in the business cycle. It has been increased during recessions, it has been increased when the economy was in the process of recovering from recessions, it has been increased before recessions, and it has been increased at times far removed from recessions. With this kind of a record, any claims that "this will happen if you increase the minimum wage" would show up as a strong statistical trend. That is, if the claims were true. "Other things going on in the economy caused those results?" When the sample includes such a wide array of circumstances, over many years, under different political philosophies, and then the results can be blamed on "other things" but never the Econ 101 claim being made, then what good is that claim for the real world?

What are the actual results of these 21 historical incidents of a minimum wage increase in the United States?

First of all, we should define what we are looking for. Are we going to look at the annual numbers for the same fiscal or calendar year that the minimum wage has increased? Are we going to look at the annual numbers for the year following the minimum wage increase, in order to allow for a time lapse for the results to work their way through the economy? Neither one of these options will show the kind of statistical correlation that would be present if the Econ 101 arguments were true. But here are the numbers for the combination of the same year's numbers and the following year's numbers:

Number of times that the minimum wage has been increased, starting in 1939: 21

Number of times that production (as measured by real GDP) has increased: 17

Number of times that production (as measured by real GDP) has decreased: 4

Number of times that the number of jobs in the economy has increased: 17

Number of times that the number of jobs in the economy has decreased: 3

(The jobs numbers add up to 20 instances instead of 21, because the data for 1939 is not available)

These numbers simply do not support a claim that an increase in the minimum wage will cost jobs or production.

Out of the 21 times that the minimum wage has been increased:

10 occurred when the economy was already experiencing recessionary forces

3 occurred shortly after the economy had recovered from a recession

2 occurred shortly before the start of a recession

6 occurred at times unrelated to a recession

Despite this historical record, under various economic conditions, the data does not support claims that an increase in the minimum wage will cause job loss. The data does not support claims that an increase in the minimum wage will cause loss of economic production.

What about the argument that an increase in the minimum wage will cause inflation, so that workers won't be any better off than before?

First of all, you have to be careful to understand exactly what inflation is, what the consequences are, and what is considered acceptable and unacceptable. The bottom line is that deflation (negative inflation, which we have experienced many times in the past) is bad for the economy; zero inflation and very low rates of inflation (such as we have now) have some of the same negative effects on the economy that deflation has, and can lead to deflation; very high rates of inflation are bad for the economy (hyperinflation is something that we have never approached despite many predictions over the years, but we have had double-digit inflation on occasion, the last time being 1981); but moderate rates of inflation are good for economic growth. Inflation rates around 3% per year are considered to be consistent with healthy economic growth; some economists would say anything between 3% and 5% is healthy.

During the time frame that a minimum wage has existed in the United States (1938 to present), there have been a total of 17 years with inflation rates above 5% (the last one was in 1990). Of these, 6 have been instances of double-digit inflation (the last one was in 1981, and all of them can be associated with either WWII or the stagflation era of the 1970s). Of the 17 times that inflation has exceeded 5%, 8 of them coincided with an increase in the minimum wage. Does this mean that an increase in the minimum wage causes inflation which leaves workers no better off than before?

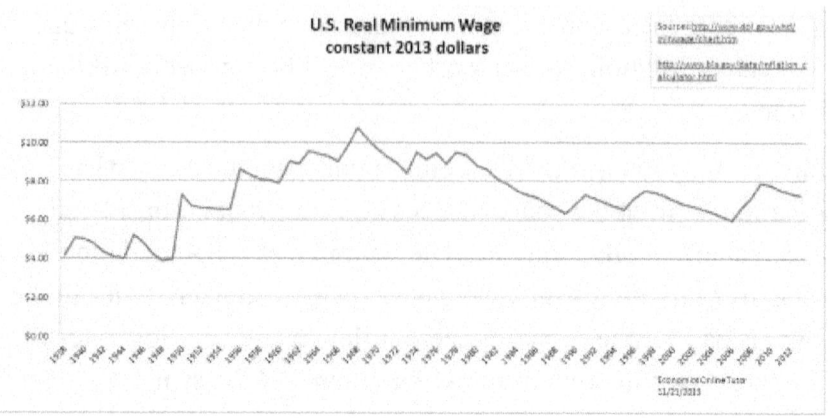

Figure 5

Figure 5 is a graph of the real minimum wage in the United States over time. This is the minimum wage adjusted for inflation. The graph shows that when the minimum wage increases, the purchasing power of a minimum wage worker increases. When the minimum wage is not increased, the purchasing power of a minimum wage worker declines over time due to normal inflation.

The real minimum wage peaked in 1968 ($10.77 per hour in 2013 dollars). It is widely acknowledged that during the time frame when the real minimum wage was higher than today's minimum wage, the average full-time worker earned a livable wage, at least compared to today's situation.

Faulty Conclusions from Teaching of Basic Economics

The historical record does not support Econ 101 claims against an increase in the minimum wage. There should be no reason to resort to citing Econ 101 teaching as a reason to oppose an increase in the minimum wage. The conclusions of the Econ 101 arguments have been shown to not hold true in the real world, so they are not valid. But why aren't they valid?

The answer lies within the Econ 101 teaching itself. The analysis of Econ 101 teaching that leads to a conclusion that "If the minimum wage is increased, this (the Unemployment Argument, the Inflation Argument, and/or the Trickle-down Argument) will happen" is not a logical argument. It ignores relevant concepts taught in a basic economics class.

The Econ 101 arguments against an increase in the minimum wage are based on conclusions from Figure 2 and Figure 4 above. However, a careful analysis of the diagrams in Figures 2 and 4 does NOT lead to a conclusion that these negative results will occur in the real world if the minimum wage is increased. What these diagrams show is that under circumstances defined by necessary assumptions, these results will occur. Such circumstances are not the same thing as the real world.

All economic models, including the basic supply & demand model in Figure 1 above, are based on a host of assumptions. Each time a model is expanded in order to add new variables, and each time a new model is introduced that is based on an earlier model, new assumptions are added. These assumptions are necessary for the models to be logically valid. But the same assumptions take the model out of the realm of the real world and place it into the laboratory-like realm of theory.

For example, Figure 6 here is the same as Figure 2 above:

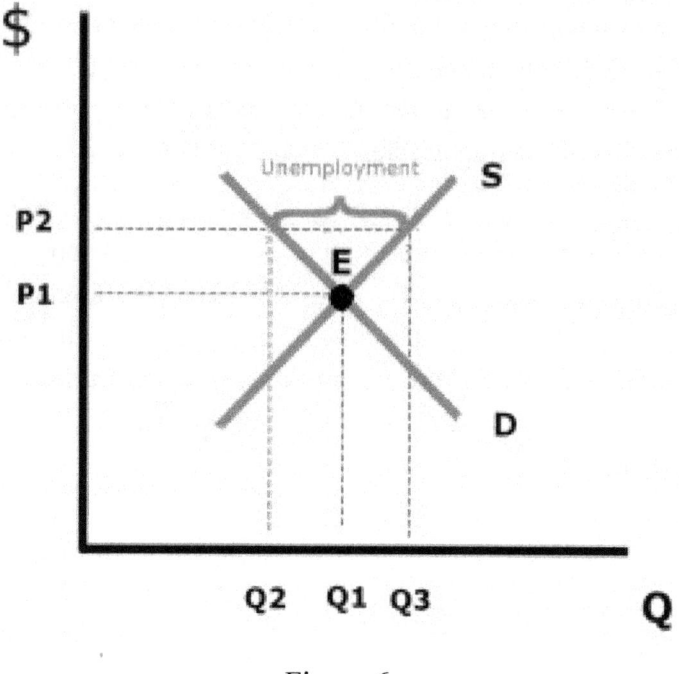

Figure 6

The Econ 101 Argument uses this model to conclude that "if the minimum wage is increased to P2, then unemployment in the amount of Q3 minus Q2 will result".

The logical form of this argument is:

If A, then X

The problem is that this is a faulty conclusion of this model. This is a model, not the real world. The model only works under a specific set of assumptions that you cannot see in the diagram. Each of these assumptions is a departure from the real world, and any valid conclusions must take the assumptions into proper consideration. Each assumption becomes an additional premise to the logical form.

Instead of:

If A, then X

The logical form of conclusions must be:

If A, and if B, and if C, and if ... N, then X

With:

X = the conclusion that is drawn, such as a specific increase in unemployment

A = the variable under consideration, such as an increase in the minimum wage

And

B, C, ... and N = all of the assumptions behind the model

The conclusions do not logically follow, unless the assumptions are included. The assumptions in turn take the model away from the realm of the real world.

*

Assumptions

The assumptions behind these models can be explicit, meaning that they might have been expressly stated as assumptions within the teaching of the models. I know that when I was a student, my professors always gave me a list of assumptions when introducing a new model. On the other hand, many of the assumptions are likely to be implicit. They have not been expressly stated as assumptions, but must be inferred from the known information. Often, implicit assumptions relate to concepts that students haven't been introduced to yet. That's one of the problems with the method that schools are teaching economics. Basic economics involves many different concepts which are interrelated, but students are introduced to them one at a time. Once new ones are introduced, there simply isn't enough time in a given course to go back through all of the previous models that the new concept applies to.

Definitions of terms involved in models are also assumptions. For example, in the supply & demand analysis used for this essay, the term "market" is important for the analysis, but so is the fact that the term is defined in a very broad, generic sense. The labor market in the analysis assumes one generic labor market which disregards different wage levels, different skill levels, different skill types, geographic limitations, and differences in the specific jobs that individuals are qualified for and interested in, among many other omissions. Inclusion of these differences would complicate the analysis, but would look more like the real world.

Supply & demand each have their own set of assumptions, which become assumptions for this analysis. The concept of elasticity, as it applies on multiple levels, is extremely important for a real-world analysis, yet ignoring elasticity is one of the assumptions being used. Supply & demand curves are included in their most generic forms, yet their properties, including slopes, are extremely important. In any given real-world labor market, however that is defined, how many more individuals would choose to enter the labor market with a given increase in the wage rate, and how much (if any) would this increase in pay induce those already in the labor market to increase hours worked and/or work harder and be more productive? There are implicit assumptions involved with all of this.

What about the part of the analysis in which supply is decreased in the product market due to an increase in the wage rate? The market equilibrium quantity and price in the product market involves many different factors. How much does a change in labor costs factor into this when there are so many other factors involved? Remember, the product market has its own equilibrium based on both the demand curve and the supply curve, and each of these curves is based on multiple factors.

One assumption in the analysis of an increase in the minimum wage is the assumption of perfect competition in all markets involved. I would guess that most students aren't even told that this is an assumption, but the analysis doesn't work without it. The direct and automatic connection between labor cost and product supply requires this assumption. It's important to note is that perfect competition doesn't even exist in the real world, and it never has. In economics classes, perfect competition is introduced as the theoretical efficiency ideal to be compared to other market structures. Each type of market is categorized into a named market structure, using another set of assumptions. In terms of properties, every market at the local level is either most closely associated with either oligopoly or monopoly, yet the analysis of the minimum wage assumes the properties associated with perfect competition. The conclusions to be drawn are completely different depending on the market structure, including the relationship between supply and labor cost.

One very important assumption is that this analysis is strictly a microeconomic analysis, with the focus entirely on the internal mechanics at the market level. Any macroeconomic effects of the microeconomic changes are specifically ignored. This is the ceteris paribus assumption. If one business increases the amount of wages it pays to its employees, then it will have a cost increase with little effect on revenue. But if the wage rate is increased across the entire economy, which it would be in the case of a minimum wage increase, then the general public will have more money to spend in retail establishments, consumer demand would increase, which would give businesses a motivation to increase production and hire more employees. This analysis includes the concept of different marginal propensities to consume (MPC) for different classifications of people, and different multiplier effects for different types of economic activities.

In terms of the type of diagrams used in the discussion above about Econ 101 arguments, the macroeconomic effects of an increase in the minimum wage in the labor market would look like this:

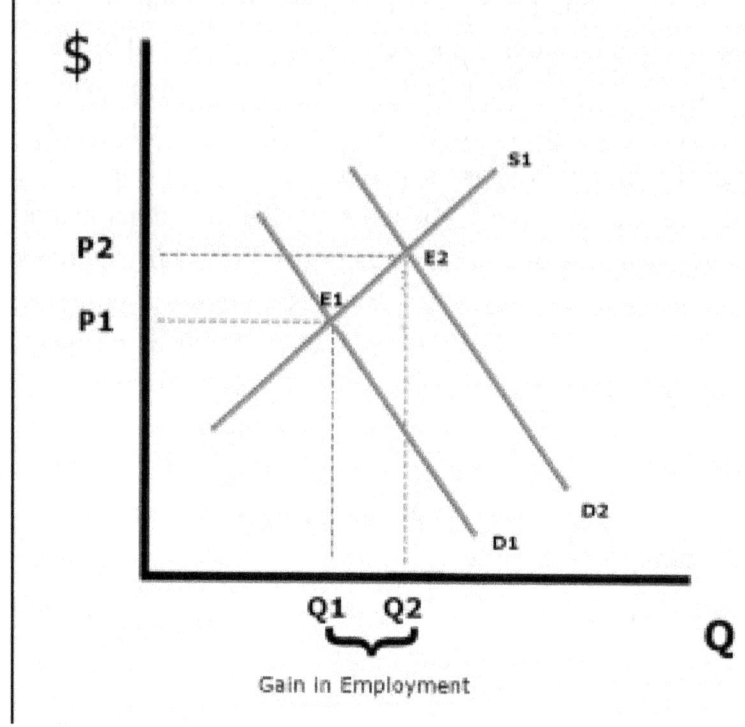

Figure 7

In figure 7, a change in the wage rate from P1 to P2 due to an increase in the minimum wage would provide consumers with additional money to spend in the economy. This will increase demand in the product markets, which would influence businesses to increase production, which would create more demand in the labor market. The additional demand in the labor market will increase, not decrease, employment. This is the opposite effect as in Figure 2 above.

I saved what is possibly the most important assumption for last. Take another look at Figure 1:

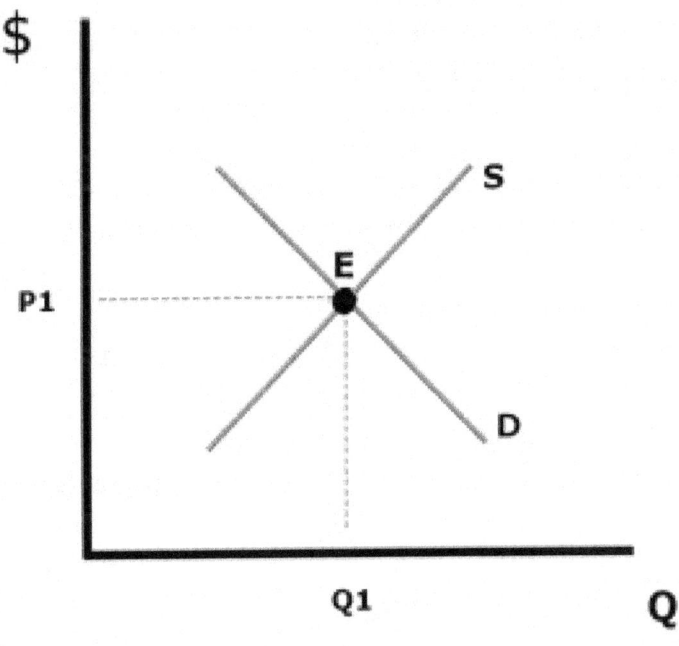

Figure 1

Left virtually unmentioned so far in this analysis is the big E where the supply and demand curves intersect. The assumption for this analysis is that this is a point of equilibrium in the given market. This assumption means that point E is the point where the market is most efficient. It implies that there are no market failures involved, the Invisible Hand is operating properly, nobody is being exploited, every choice to enter or not enter the market is voluntary, no asymmetrical information exists, and each side in every transaction has equal market power. In other words, everything is hunky-dory in this market. Since markets are interrelated, everything is hunky-dory in all related markets.

This assumption that E = all of the above characteristics is vital to the conclusions in the Econ 101 arguments that an increase in the minimum wage will have specific negative effects on individuals and on the economy. The entire set of conclusions is invalid if this assumption is not true.

In reality, point E is none of the above. This point is merely the beginning point, the "before" in a "before" and "after" analysis of a policy change.

Take a look at the labor market today. Take a look at the history of the labor market. Do you honestly believe that each side has equal market power? If you believe in free market theory, then you have to know that in free markets, labor is supposed to be paid according to productivity. Yet there has been a divergence of wages and productivity ever since policy changes have overwhelmingly favored employers at the expense of employees. Wages haven't gone up, in real terms, for over 30 years now, yet productivity has continued along the same upward path. Labor is receiving a smaller share than it used to. People are working full time for less-than-living wages. Employed people are forced to apply for public assistance because their employers are not paying them enough to survive. There are many long-term unemployed people, and many of those who do have jobs are working for poverty wages.

Clearly, this is a case of market failure. This subject is also covered in an Econ 101 course, but is not mentioned by those who invoke an Econ 101 argument against an increase in the minimum wage. What does Econ 101 say about correcting for this type of market failure?

Take a look at Figure 8 below.

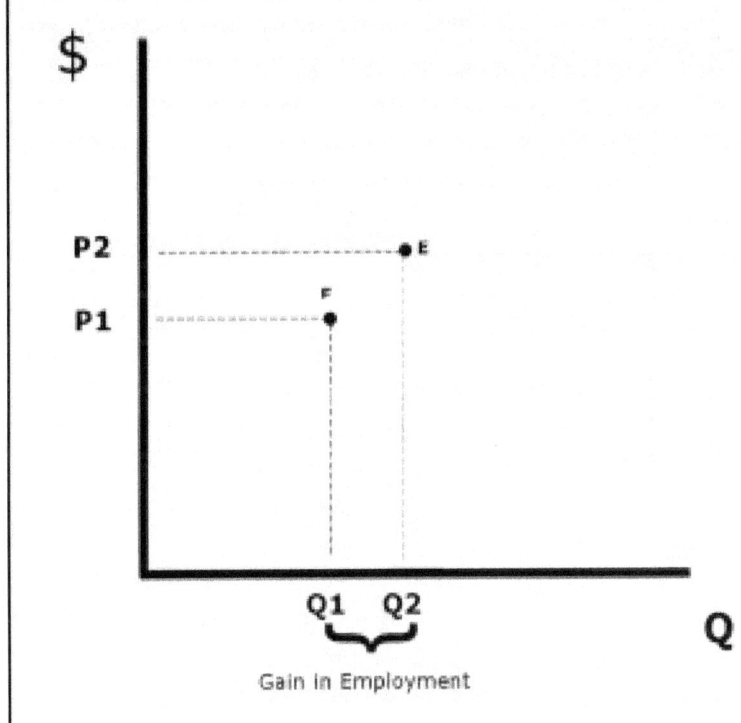

Figure 8

Suppose you could convince policymakers that the labor market is operating at point F, but due to market failure, the economy would work better if it were operating at point E. Point E has a higher wage rate for workers, and there are more people with jobs. How do you go from point F to point E? According to Econ 101, in order to correct for market failure by increasing both price and quantity, you need to increase demand.

A diagram of a correction, with the appropriate supply & demand curves, would look like this:

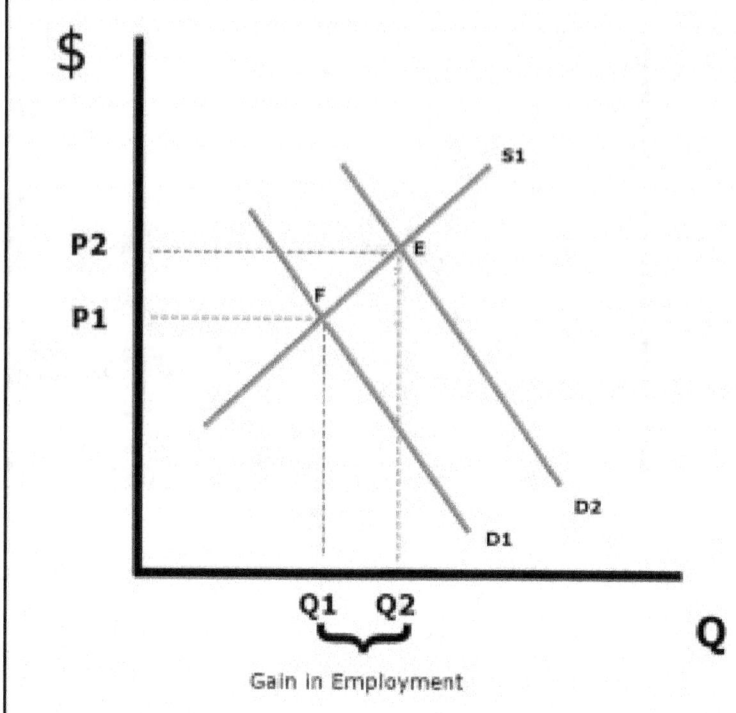

Figure 9

This would be an Econ 101 correction for market failure. It would move the market from a position of failure (point F) to a position of market equilibrium (point E). And how do we do that?

We've already been there in this analysis. Look above. Figure 9, the correction for market failure, is identical to Figure 7 above, the effects including macroeconomic effects of an increase in the minimum wage!

This analysis is consistent with the historical record. It is consistent with concepts taught in Econ 101 class, including the concepts ignored by those who invoke the Econ 101 arguments to argue for a completely different conclusion. The main difference, in terms of the types of diagrams that the Econ 101 arguments are based, is the difference between calling the current situation optimal or not optimal.

The Econ 101 arguments against an increase in the minimum wage require the current situation to be considered optimal.

Section 10: Budgets, Deficits and Government Debt

"The U.S. Government Always Balances its Budget" – page 157

The U.S. Government Always Balances its Budget

(Originally published August 4, 2014 for The Blue Route Blog)

The U.S. government does not run a budget deficit, ever. It's true. When the bills come due, the bills get paid. The federal government never defaults on its obligations. The only thing that can prevent a balanced budget would be if Congress refused to increase the debt limit.

You might be saying right now, "How absurd! This is idiotic! Of course the government doesn't balance its budget every year. The bills get paid because the government increases its debt, not because the government takes in enough revenue. They just print more money. That is not balancing the budget!"

Okay, you have a point. But I have a point to make also. I used an absurd statement in order to point out some equally-absurd statements against allowing the government to run a deficit. My original statement is false because a budget is not balanced if total revenue isn't enough to cover total expenditures. It is important to note that total expenditures include payments for current expenses as well as contracts entered into for future payments to be made. If you only count payments made as they come due, then my statement would be correct. The United States government has always paid its obligations when they come due. The United States government does have a history of never running a budget deficit, if you count the bills when they come due instead of counting when the obligations are entered into.

But that isn't what we are talking about when we discuss the budget deficit. The budget deficit is based on future obligations entered into, not on current bills due. With one definition of a deficit (my original one above), the United States never runs a deficit. But with the commonly-used definition of a deficit, we get a different story. The historical fact is that the U.S. government rarely balances its budget.

Keep this in mind. A deficit occurs when obligations for future payments are incurred. That is the definition of a deficit we are using when we discuss the government's budget.

By the same token, and using the same definition, households and businesses don't always balance their budgets either. I have used an absurd statement about the government balancing its budget, by using an alternative definition of what a budget is, in order to make a point about equally absurd political rhetoric used to equate government spending with household and business spending.

When a household puts anything on credit that doesn't get paid off right away, it is running a deficit – if you use the same definition for a deficit that you are using when you discuss a government deficit. When people take out mortgages to be paid off over a long period of time; when they take on car payments, credit card payments, student loans, bank loans, and any other obligation where the entire obligation is not paid off in the same year, then they are running a deficit – if you use the same definition for a deficit. Households run deficits the same way the government runs a deficit.

Businesses routinely use credit. Not just to cover start-up costs, major expansions, and unexpected catastrophes, but for a host of other reasons. Large businesses hire expensive tax attorneys and accountants to tell them when and how to leverage, when increasing debt is in their best interest. Using the same definition that you use for government, businesses don't always balance their budgets either.

The federal government covers its budget shortfall by offering treasury securities for sale to the public. The public buys these up because they are considered the safest investments in the entire world. Even when the ratings agencies decided to downgrade these securities, the prices went up because the public trusts these investments and the ratings don't matter. What becomes debt for the government is an investment for investors, and a very popular one. And the U.S. has never defaulted on this debt.

The point I am trying to make is this:

Statements such as…

"Government deficits are wrong because we the people always have to live within our budgets; and the government should too."

and

"Government deficits are wrong because businesses have to pay their bills and the government should too."

…are simply invalid arguments. Those are meaningless words, but people make those kinds of statements all the time.

Those kinds of statements can only be true if you take the same definition of deficits that I used for the government when I made the claim that the government never runs a deficit, and apply it to households and businesses; while at the same time, use a different definition for the same term and apply it to the government. Applying a different definition for deficits to the government than you do to households and businesses, and then making arguments as if they are the same things, is an inconsistent comparison, a type of non sequitur logical fallacy. It simply is not valid. The statement that I made above, that the government always balances its budget, is false. I only made that statement in order to point out the equally absurd argument that the government should be forced to balance its budget every year because households and businesses have to.

I could stop right here. I have made my point. But if I leave it at this, I can just see a lot of people saying something like "he just said that deficits are always good." No, I did not say that. Don't read something that is not here into what I am saying and then argue against what you are reading into it. Doing so would be a straw man argument; also invalid.

I also did not say that the government is the same as a household or a business. I said that the definition of a deficit should be consistently applied when comparing governments, households, and businesses. But I did not say that these entities are the same. There are important differences when it comes to the wisdom of deficit spending. Important similarities also exist.

First, the similarities: Think in terms of opportunity cost. Debt, whether undertaken by individuals, households, businesses, or governments, is undertaken for the purpose of gaining something. It is a trade-off. If the benefits of any specific instance of deficit spending outweigh the costs, relative to other options, then adding to debt would be a wise choice. If the costs outweigh the benefits, then doing so would not be wise. If a different option creates a better net benefit, then deficit spending is not wise. The true cost of any decision is the opportunity cost. Deficit spending is an investment in the future, and this investment can be wise or unwise. For many people, the debt associated with a mortgage is a wise trade-off for home ownership. Many other people choose never to go into debt. They choose to pay for everything out of money that they have already received. The trade-off for these people is a limited ability to make large-ticket purchases as well as a limited ability to increase their standard of living. Unless somebody gives them a large sum of money somewhere, most people cannot increase their standard of living very much without taking on some debt somewhere along the line. Debt can be looked on as an investment in the future, so deciding to forgo debt means forgoing that particular investment. The same thing can be said for government spending. The wisdom of each choice is not clear until all of the costs and benefits have been factored in – on a case by case basis.

But there are important differences. One obvious difference is that the federal government gets to print its own money. Also, the government gets to make the rules. These facts can make adding to debt seem less painful for the government in the short run. It means that the government could have incentives to add to debt without a full cost/benefit analysis. But it does not mean that government debt is always bad, and that the cost of debt to taxpayers is always higher than the benefits. It does mean that we as taxpayers need to be vigilant. We need to be fully aware of all potential costs and benefits. For example, there are safeguards in place that are designed to give the government an incentive to make these decisions based on net benefit. The big-picture benefits to shoot for are even defined for the government. Do you know what these safeguards are, which ways they work, and which ways they fail? Do you know the historical record of the economic outcomes of various spending decisions?

I'll mention one other important difference. Households consume goods and services. Businesses produce goods and services. The U.S. government does neither. Spending means different things for these three types of entities. Because of this, the costs and benefits are going to be different.

"Wait", you may say. Government spending IS consumption. No, it isn't, not when you are doing a cost/benefit analysis based on opportunity costs. When the government spends, it is acting as sort of a middleman for the private sector. Everything that the government does affects both consumption and production in the private sector. These effects can be huge. They can be negative effects. But they also can be positive effects. Government services provide the means for private industry and the economy to function. Government activities can mitigate and even reverse the negative effects of a recession.

All government actions affect the economy. These actions can have positive effects, and they can have negative effects. Each situation is different. It is up to citizens to monitor their government and hold it responsible. But this requires a cost/benefit analysis of individual situations. It doesn't serve any useful purpose to make a simplistic statement such as "the government is always the problem" or "the private sector can do everything that the government can do, only better". Those kinds of statements might have strong political and emotional appeal, but they are extremely easy to prove false. Attempts to justify them usually involve arguments of sweeping generalization as well as ad nauseam, both logical fallacies. Sweeping generalization means that an obvious conclusion reached from some specific situation is used as evidence that the same specific conclusion will "always" result in every other situation. Ad nauseam means that the same line, the same truism, is repeated over and over again until people hear them so often that they come to the conclusion that the statements must be true – so these people ignore the real evidence to the contrary.

Government spending can and does have positive aspects, but also negative aspects. It makes sense to look at these aspects for specific situations. It does not make sense to avoid looking at the real costs and benefits by making fallacious sweeping generalizations. Part of the cost/benefit analysis for government spending involves the decision to pay for expenditures with current tax revenue (and the decision on how and from whom to raise this revenue) or to pay for expenditures with additional debt. Each one of these options has its own advantages and disadvantages, and just as in the private sector, a combination of current revenue and new debt can be the best answer.

What about the idea of lowering total government spending just for its own sake? What about austerity as an economic policy?

Apply the same kind of cost/benefit analysis. Do you know the actual results, the costs and benefits, from opposing policies in various situations? There is a very long historical record on this; do you know what it is? Do you know the difference between the statements of simplicity, the rhetoric, and the actual record? There is no need to cite old theories based on controlled circumstances that do not exist in the real world; there is an actual real-world record. And in cases where the Constitution is mentioned in the arguments as a reason to oppose government debt of any kind, or government spending for certain kinds of expenditures (such as general welfare), do you know the difference between the rhetoric and the actual wording of the Constitution?

Section 11: Social Security and Welfare

Some Important Truths about the Future of Social Security

(Originally published August 26, 2014 for The Blue Route Blog)

This essay will cover and explain all of the following issues in order:

A. What people claim to be true about Social Security's insolvency

B. Separating the truth from the rhetoric

C. Analyzing proposed solutions to perceived solvency issues

***

Something seems to be wrong with this picture:

The Social Security system began in 1937. Every year between 1937 and 2010, the system took in more money in Social Security tax receipts than it paid out in benefits. For each year, some 73 years, the excess funds had been invested in high-grade U.S. Treasury securities. That's 73 years of compound earnings – surely enough to cover a shortfall created when we have a generation in which the working age percentage of the population decreases and the percentage of the population receiving Social Security increases. This is something that is going to happen in cycles, and it is what has happened in recent years. The baby-boomers started reaching retirement age, meaning that a generation with a large population began receiving Social Security benefits while a generation with a relatively smaller population paid taxes into the system. If the formula for determining how much tax to collect is calculated properly, then this normal cycle in demographics should be no big deal. The excess funds in the Social Security Trust Fund, comprised of 73 years of excess tax collections along with interest compounded over the years, should cover this. Then, when the demographic cycle starts to repeat itself, the trust fund will begin to grow again. The reason to even have excess funds is to cover this expected change in demographics. The balance goes up, then the balance goes down, and then the cycle starts again, all the while there is plenty of money in the trust fund to cover benefit payments.

Yet we are being told that Social Security is in a crisis right now. It is no longer solvent. How can that be? Why aren't the excess funds enough to cover the baby-boomers in their retirement years?

There have been some big changes in the Social Security system over the years. Many more people are covered than they were in 1937. Instead of a simple retirement system, it has become a safety net for certain surviving spouses, as well as a system to pay benefits to disabled persons and their dependent children. There have been adjustments for inflation, which look huge when you look backwards over a long period of time. But at the same time, there have been adjustments made to the formula for collecting taxes; adjustments that are designed to cover any changes in benefits in order to keep the system solvent. If the formula that has been used is the correct one, and if Congress has applied that formula properly, then there should always be enough excess funds to keep the system solvent – even for periods of time in which the benefit payments exceed the tax collections. But we are told it is no longer solvent, and we have to make drastic changes NOW. How can that be?

We have heard a lot of stories.

The government has raided the Social Security Trust Fund in order to hide deficit spending elsewhere in the budget.

The government has raided the Social Security Trust Fund in order to finance wars "off the books" (say liberals), or to pay for out-of-control spending on social programs (say conservatives).

The government takes money from the Social Security Trust Fund and uses it for general expenditures.

The government issues an IOU to Social Security but has no intention of repaying what it owes.

Social Security is supposed to be a simple retirement system and should never have grown into something else.

People are simply living longer past retirement age, and receiving benefits for more years.

Social Security is nothing but a Ponzi scheme.

Social Security is an entitlement that is breaking the federal budget.

If we don't cut benefits now, Social Security will go broke.

Our children will have nothing because today's Social Security recipients are draining the funds.

*

There are many different stories of problems and dire predictions coming from all directions. What is the truth? Is this a crisis situation that we must fix right now? What are the real problems, and how do we fix them? Take note of the above list of perceived problems. We will return to it shortly in this discussion.

First of all, we have a language barrier to overcome. Many of these stories are based on truths that can be countered with other truths that tell the same story from a different perspective, and each perspective will lead you towards a completely different conclusion. The same concepts are told in different ways by different people in an attempt to gain sympathy for a particular point. What we need to do is get rid of these half-truths, and narrow the focus to the "real truths" – a term that I am using for truths void of any rhetorical and misleading language – in other words, truths that are relevant facts which aren't simply restatements of opposing facts.

For example, "the excess funds have been invested in high-grade U.S. Treasury securities" and "the government has raided the Social Security Trust Fund in order to hide deficit spending elsewhere in the budget" are two completely opposing views of the exact same event. The connotations of the exact same occurrence are completely different depending on the language used. We can't have a reasonable discussion of what is going on, and how to fix it, unless we focus on the "real truths" and leave the misleading language out of it. If one person says something that can be construed as a fact, but somebody else can say something that is almost the exact opposite yet still is a fact, then we end up arguing over "facts" that are mere rhetorical talking points.

I'll discuss the items on the above list of stories that we are hearing about the demise of Social Security, separating the rhetoric and misleading connotations from the 'real truths". But first, it will be helpful to point out exactly what the Social Security system is.

In broad terms, Social Security is a system in which benefits are paid to retirees, certain spouses of retirees, disabled persons, dependent children of disabled persons, and survivors of beneficiaries. These benefits are financed through withholding taxes.

Of course, this is only a broad explanation. There are many details, but listing them here would distract from the purpose of this writing. Some of the details, though, are important to a discussion of the current problems and what should be done to fix the problems. I'll mention those details below, as they relate to proposed solutions.

Now, go back to the "we have heard a lot of stories" section above. Here are the points listed, along with a discussion of what they mean in terms of "real facts" void of misleading language.

The government has raided the Social Security Trust Fund in order to hide deficit spending elsewhere in the budget.

The government has raided the Social Security Trust Fund in order to finance wars "off the books" (say liberals), or to pay for out-of-control spending on social programs (say conservatives).

The government takes money from the Social Security Trust Fund and uses it for general expenditures.

The government issues an IOU to Social Security but has no intention of repaying what it owes.

These are different ways to talk about the same process. The language used in each represents a specific viewpoint, not a separate "real truth".

The Social Security Trust Fund is a huge fund from which future benefits are to be paid. As of the end of 2013, the balance in this fund was $2.76 trillion. This balance represents the cumulative receipts of Social Security taxes over the years, plus interest earned on the balance, minus benefits already paid. Interest is earned because the fund balance is invested in U.S. Treasury securities, considered by most finance professionals to be the safest investments in the world. From the point of view of the Social Security Administration, this is simply an investment. The different points of view come about when you look at these transactions in terms of what they mean to the Treasury Department which issues these securities, as well what they mean to the federal budget.

To the government, the funds invested in Treasury Securities represent loan proceeds. That's how the bond market always works. Those who invest are loaning money to those who issue bonds. It happens with corporate bonds, and it happens with government bonds. From the point of view of Social Security, the money is an investment. From the point of view of Treasury, the money is a loan receipt. This is government debt, but it is also a government asset – available cash. This means that the money that Social Security invests for its fund is at the same time money available to the government for general purposes. It is also a relatively cheap way for the government to finance debt, since Treasury securities have low interest rates.

The national debt is simply a cumulative balance of all outstanding Treasury securities. Approximately 2/3 of the debt is listed as "debt held by the public". The other 1/3 is listed as "debt held by other government agencies". The amount owed to Social Security falls into this latter category – indeed, Social Security makes up the largest share of this kind of debt. Without funds from Social Security, the government would have to get the funds elsewhere – some combination of tax increases and more government debt in the category of "debt held by the public". This includes debt held by foreign entities.

I should add a disclaimer of sorts here. I was motivated to write an essay on this topic after reading, and receiving permission to use, an essay from an economics professor who insists that there are no real Treasury securities involved, at least for the amount of the 1983 Social Security tax increase. In 1983, the increase in social security taxes more than offset the 1981 decrease in income taxes for the middle class, making Reagan's tax reforms a net tax increase for the working class. This professor claims that only paper IOUs have been issued; and that no repayment, including interest, has been made or is intended to ever be made. If true, then this would indeed represent a "raiding" of Social Security. However, my subsequent research could not confirm his claims. His position seems to be based in part on isolated comments from members of Congress. I grew suspicious of his claims when I could not find any facts to back them up; when I found numerous sources that I consider to be reliable which supported what I wrote above but did not support the professor's claims; and especially when the amount he listed as being the amount raided since 1983 happened to be the same amount as the entire Social Security Trust Fund balance.

Stay tuned. If he is proven to be correct, this will become a huge story. It would make much of my analysis here irrelevant. I have chosen not to list his name, nor plug his book as he requested, because my research could not support his claims.

Social Security is supposed to be a simple retirement system and should never have grown into something else.

I'm not sure what point this claim is supposed to be making. What Social Security used to be, or what it was originally intended to be, is completely irrelevant to its problems now, unless it can be shown that people in general would be better off if Social Security had not evolved. Without the "better off" points of a previous version of Social Security, this is not a valid argument. If the "better off" points are included, then those points can be compared on a cost/benefit basis to competing claims. Simply stating "what used to be" is not an argument for "what should be now". That Social Security is a different type of system than it used to be is a fact, but not a "real truth" in terms of relevancy.

It is true that Social Security was originally a much smaller and simpler system. It was a "social insurance program of focusing on low and middle-income workers who were more likely to be economically vulnerable in retirement".

That is why it was designed to be financed through withholding taxes based on wages from jobs, and not financed through other means. That is why there was an income cap for withholding – the system itself was designed to be focused on those who were vulnerable, not those with high earnings. It is difficult to find, through research, any compelling reason for an income limit on withholding, other than the fact that the original focus of the entire system was on the working poor and middle class. Although the system has evolved into a broader collection of benefits, and has become an important part of the overall economy, today's arguments for retaining an income cap are similar to the arguments back then. "The rich don't receive the benefits, so the rich shouldn't have to pay to support the system." I personally do not agree with that argument – not when everybody benefits from the economic advantages of having a solvent Social Security system in place. It can be argued that in a real sense, Social Security has evolved into an important part of the nation's infrastructure – even if that was not the original intention.

People are simply living longer past retirement age, receiving benefits for more years.

This is also a fact. But is it a "real truth" as an argument regarding how to fix social security? Consider this, which is also a fact: Very recently, for the first time, people began receiving less money, in lifetime benefits, than they paid into the system during their entire working lives. That's right. People are getting less out of it than they paid into it. They paid taxes throughout their working careers, and perhaps they expected to get that money back, plus interest, after they retired. Yet due to rules in place, people are not outliving the money that they paid into the system. They are adding to, not depleting, the fund balance, even during a time when they are living longer. This is a recent development. When it comes to arguments over whether to reduce monthly benefits or increase the retirement age, we have two competing facts: One, people are

172

living longer; but two, they will not get back what they put into the system. Two competing facts; what is the "real truth"?

Social Security is nothing but a Ponzi scheme.

Well, no it isn't. This kind of argument doesn't say what is wrong with the system, other than to imply that: "Social Security's problems are the problems of a Ponzi scheme – and hey, everybody knows that a Ponzi scheme is evil, so that makes the Social Security system itself evil, so let's just get rid of it – and by the way, since it is evil, there is no need to try to discuss this issue rationally; therefore, end of discussion."

That is what such a claim seems to be designed to imply. But Social Security is not a Ponzi scheme. Saying that it is relies on a definition of a Ponzi scheme that does not require any of the "evils" that are implied in the arguments against Social Security.

Social Security is an entitlement that is breaking the federal budget.

Social Security's funding is direct. The money that goes into the trust fund comes from payroll taxes that are dedicated for a specific purpose. It is separate from the federal government's general fund. The fact that Social Security only invests in Treasury securities means that the government gets funds for its budget through a government agency source. It actually adds revenue to the federal budget, decreasing the amount of bonds that the Treasury needs to sell on the open market. This means less upward pressure on interest rates, cutting the government's interest costs. It also means less "ownership" of the federal government by foreigners. Social Security is not breaking the federal budget.

What about the other part of that statement. Is Social Security an entitlement? Here is an example of a fact that is different from a "real truth". Whoever says that Social Security is an entitlement is stating a fact. Social Security is an entitlement. But why would that fact even matter, why would it even be mentioned, in an argument over Social Security's problems? I can only think of one reason, and that is to take advantage of some unfair negative connotations behind the word "entitlement".

Social Security is an entitlement for one reason only. It is an entitlement because the money is being held for somebody else's future use. Somebody will be entitled to it in the future; that's why it is an entitlement. The false negative connotations are that somehow, this is money that is going from hard-working taxpayers and given to freeloaders. That is not what an entitlement is, but that is what people have been led to believe due to misinformation through political rhetoric. That is also not what Social Security is, but by using language that implies otherwise, calling Social Security an entitlement falsely associates Social Security with negative connotations.

If we don't cut benefits now, Social Security will go broke. Our children will have nothing because today's Social Security recipients are draining the funds.

This is what the current "we have to do something now" argument is all about. It is why this is even an issue today.

This would be a good time to take a look at where Social Security currently stands financially.

The Social Security Trust Fund currently has a huge balance, $2.76 trillion as of the beginning of the year. That is more than the total of all income taxes, individual and corporate, paid in the United States in one year. For about 73 years since its inception, Social Security had taken in more than it paid out. But since 2010, it has paid out more than it has taken in. The most recent projections from the Congressional Budget Office (CBO) and others indicate that unless changes are made, within 19 years the fund will be about 23% short of being able to pay 100% of the benefits that it is projected to owe. In 1960, there were 4.9 workers for every beneficiary; in 2012, there were only 2.8 workers per beneficiary, and the CBO projects that in 2035 there will only be 1.9 workers per beneficiary. In 1960, the typical family could expect to receive 7 times in benefits what they paid into the system. Today, they pay more than they receive. Today, 6 million Americans over the age of 65 are living in poverty. That number is projected to be 33% higher by the year 2020.

Those are the relevant facts as we know them, the "real truths" of the current situation. For the most part, the arguments, the rhetoric, and the proposed fixes stem from these few facts.

A number of events and trends have been cited as contributors to a change from a system that takes in more than it pays out, to a system that is said to be no longer solvent.

The baby-boomer generation is reaching retirement age.

People are living longer than they used to.

There has been an increase in the number and types of benefits.

The income cap no longer captures enough income to cover projected payouts, due to increased income inequality.

Cost of living adjustments mean more money being paid out.

The formula for determining the tax rate and the income gap is wrong or has been misapplied by Congress.

You might have noticed that some of the known and relevant facts cited above are future projections. For example, it isn't a fact that Social Security will have a shortfall within 19 years – it is only a fact that Social Security is *projected* to have such a shortfall. What if the projections are wrong? Some of the contributing factors to the current situation are changes in demographics – namely, the existence of a baby-boomer generation that is reaching retirement age. The CBO and other projections are based on assumptions of future demographics. What if they are wrong? The number 19, as in 19 years until Social Security won't be able to pay full benefits, is an interesting number. That is the number of years that it takes a person to advance from conception to working age. These projections are based on the number of workers we will have, and some of them haven't even been born yet. How do they know how many of them there will be? How do they know how many working-age immigrants we will have, or what our immigration policy will look like? The CBO bases its projections on taking current law and current trends, and extending them into the future. Yet trends do not tend to remain constant over long periods of time.

Proposed Solutions

1. Do nothing now

The argument for doing nothing goes something like this: There is no current crisis. There is only a projection of a future shortfall under current trends. It makes no sense to cut benefits now, in order to avoid the possibility of having to cut benefits 19 years down the road. Wait, see if the projections pan out, and deal with the problem when we know that it really is a problem. Why do something now because we are afraid that we might have to do the same thing later?

2. Eliminate the entire program or privatize

This argument is popular with many conservatives. It fits in nicely with the "government is always the problem" and "the private sector can do everything better than the government" rhetoric. But it isn't going to happen. Social Security is here to stay. It has become an important part of the nation's infrastructure, and important to the national interest. That alone means that the federal government is the proper authority for running the program. It provides many benefits for many different individuals who are financially vulnerable. It is popular, even among conservatives. While many conservatives are saying we should eliminate or privatize Social Security, many others are saying "don't cut benefits for old people!"

Privatization would impose additional administrative costs as well as add a level of profits to the cost of participants. And who would be the participants? The system won't work as it is designed to if participation is voluntary. If we keep it mandatory, then privatization would mean paperwork for every wage earner and beneficiary in order to prove that they are paying a private company to do something that the government has always done. And perhaps most important to many people, privatization does not address the specific problems within the system.

3. Invest in the stock market

This is a version of privatization that has gained a lot of traction among many people. It addresses the dwindling trust fund issue by creating a trust fund with much higher earnings potential.

Social Security is only allowed to invest in high-grade U.S. Treasury securities. These securities are extremely safe, which means that their yields do not include any risk premium. They pay very low interest compared to alternative investments. Over long periods of time, such as the entire working age of someone who is paying into Social Security, the yields on stocks are much higher than the yields on Treasuries. So why not allow Social Security to invest in the stocks of U.S. corporations?

An interesting side note on this subject is the fact that when Social Security was being proposed by FDR in 1935, investing in stocks was one of the details under consideration. The idea was rejected because doing so would be considered socialism. It would mean the government would own pieces of private businesses, in essence picking winners and losers based on which stocks they purchased for the Social Security Trust Fund. I find it interesting that many of the people who support investing Social Security funds in the stock market also scream "Socialism!" as a reason to reject government policies that they don't like.

Investing Social Security funds in the stock market would add many costs and negative consequences to the economy.

It wouldn't be popular. If the government simply invested all of the trust fund into one stock fund, then people's entire future will hinge on the ups and downs of the stock market. What kind of fund would it be: would it focus on blue chip stocks, would it focus on income stocks, would it focus on growth stocks? Would it be a mixed fund, with some bonds and even Treasury securities included? Different types of funds are advisable for different groups of individuals. Based on the historic record, and there is no guarantee of future earnings, growth stocks are best for someone who won't have to worry about collecting benefits for a long time. But somebody near retirement, or in retirement if the money stays in the same fund until collected, can be wiped out by an untimely drop in stock prices. Most people do not want to take such a risk, and if forced to do so would be living in fear for their financial security.

What if, instead of one fund for all, the government allowed people to choose between different funds, and re-allocate funds at various times? What if the government allowed people to choose between the traditional Treasury-only fund and one or more stock funds? In other words, let individuals decide for themselves?

This would impose tremendous costs on the system. What we are talking about is a system where current retirees, and those who retire in the near future, must continue to be paid while everybody else is allowed to have a fund whose earnings reflect the true results of their investment choices. In other words, two separate types of accounts, which together add up to a large increase in promised benefits, must be maintained until every current beneficiary dies. This cannot be done without very large transition costs spread out over the lifetime of today's retirees. Where is this money going to come from, and are those who propose this solution willing to accept these costs?

But giving people such a choice will not be popular, even if we can deal with the huge cost issue. Many people don't want choices, they want security; many people don't want paperwork forced on them, they want freedom; many people don't want to become or to hire financial experts, they want simplicity.

Besides, each of the various types of stock market alternatives for Social Security is further complicated by the existence of different types of beneficiaries: not just retirees are involved, but also disabled persons, spouses, children, and survivors.

4. Cut the rate of inflation

The idea behind this sounds straightforward. Without inflation, benefit payments won't have to be increased due to an increase in the cost of living. Future benefit payments can be cut without decreasing the standard of living for our retirees. This will cut the amount of benefits paid out, and will prolong the solvency of the Social Security Trust Fund.

But this isn't what it appears to be.

Policies designed specifically to cut inflation will not only backfire in their attempt to shore up Social Security, they will do much harm to the economy in the process.

The actual inflation rate is the average of all price changes. All prices do not change at the same rate. Some prices go down while others are going up. Inflation is the average. The rate of inflation as published is not the actual inflation rate, but rather a calculation based on several assumptions about American demographics. Individual price changes affect different groups of people to different degrees. The economic reason for prices to change constantly, but not together, is a constant reallocation of resources. When the general trend in prices is upward, it often means that an increase in demand has strained resources, and that unemployment is low. When the general trend of prices is not upward, it often means that resources are being unused, that the economy is underperforming, and that unemployment is high.

A low level of price inflation is considered by economists to be good for the economy. Economic growth won't take place without it. If you look back at price changes over a long period of time, the changes look very big. But if you look at average changes per year, they are not big at all – they are consistent with economic growth.

Policies designed to decrease inflation create two major problems for the economy. One, they bring us closer to deflation, which is much worse for the economy than normal inflation.

Two, they work through cuts in wages. When policy-makers talk about cutting inflation, they are specifically looking at ways to cut wages, using the theory that consumer price cuts will follow wage cuts in a market economy. These policies are not designed to give workers an increase in the standard of living. As for Social Security, wage cuts mean fewer payroll taxes being collected, decreasing the amount of deposits into the trust fund. They will not shore up the trust fund.

5. Switch to a chained-CPI

This is another idea designed to decrease future benefit payments. This proposal is being fought over in Washington right now. The idea behind it is that the CPI measure being used to calculate cost of living adjustments (COLA) overstates the rate of inflation for retirees, providing them with an annual increase in benefits which exceeds any increase in their cost of living. This is obviously wrong, and it is based on cherry-picking certain drawbacks of the regular CPI measurement.

The concept of switching to the chained-CPI measurement for determining the COLA for retirees requires a belief that senior citizens are increasing their purchasing power each year because their annual SS increases are greater than their inflation-related increases in living expenses. It doesn't take a genius to know such a belief isn't true.

6 Increase the retirement age

This is already being done, but there are proposals to increase the retirement age even more. This is a proposal to help shore up the trust fund through a decrease in future benefit payments. The justification is that people on average are living longer than they used to, and are active at an older age – so they are capable of working. Instead of receiving benefits and therefore taking money out of the system, people affected by this change would be paying into the system.

People on average are living longer, but at the same time they have begun to pay more into the system than they can expect to get out of it in terms of benefits. Increasing the retirement age would mean that the discrepancy between what they pay into it and what they get out of it would increase.

Besides, there is a form of ecological fallacy involved here. People on average are living longer than before, and on average may be capable of working at an older age than people used to be able to. But those are averages. Is it right to use these averages to force each individual to work until a later age? What is true statistically for a large group of people might not be true for each individual in that group.

7 Increase the withholding tax rate

The idea behind this proposal is to adjust the formula for calculating the solvency of the Social Security Trust Fund. This method has been used throughout the history of Social Security. When Social Security was first implemented in 1937, the employees and employers each chipped in 1% of wages. Today, each chips in 6.2%, with self-employed individuals paying 12.4%. The last increase was in 1990.

Each increase in the tax rate, of course, decreases the take-home pay of workers while increasing the labor costs for employers. Payroll taxes (Social Security and Medicare) now account for one-third of all federal revenue.

8. Comprehensive immigration reform

It is unlikely that immigration reform alone will fix what is wrong with Social Security, but it could help. The idea behind this proposal is that one of the causes of a shortfall in the trust fund is fewer workers supporting more beneficiaries, due to demographic changes. A well-designed immigration system could work to offset these demographic changes by bringing in more workers who will pay into the system.

This one isn't politically popular at a time when long-term unemployment is high, even though it can be shown that immigrants' role as consumers actually create more jobs than they take away from people who are already here.

Even though this idea currently isn't popular, it could help alleviate the problem, especially if immigration reform is viewed as one part of a larger economic development policy.

9. Raise or eliminate the income cap

Just like the proposal to increase the Social Security tax rate, the idea behind this proposal is to adjust the formula for calculating the solvency of the Social Security Trust Fund. But this one could actually solve the entire solvency issue all by itself, without causing undue damage to the economy. Many economists support this idea.

I've mentioned this proposal earlier in this essay. The income cap for Social Security tax withholding goes back to the original idea of Social Security being limited to a retirement fund for vulnerable low and middle class workers. Only those classes were considered in determining both the funding and benefits. Since then, Social Security has not only grown into a program with multiple benefits, but also has become an integral part of our economy and our infrastructure. Yet, the cap remains, without any justification other than the justification that was used for the original, limited system.

The cap has been increased numerous times over the years. Originally, it was raised whenever Congress took action to raise it. In more recent times, it is raised automatically based on a formula. The cap currently stands at 117,000. Nobody has to pay Social Security taxes on salary income exceeding $117,000. Those who make less than $117,000 pay Social Security taxes on all wage income, making this tax regressive.

The cap has failed to cover enough income to maintain the same degree of solvency for the Social Security system as it once did. The formula that is used for determining the cap is based on average wages. But in recent decades, trickle-down policies in Washington have led to a much wider income gap. A much higher percentage of all income is exempt from the tax because it is going to people whose incomes exceed the cap. The income gap doesn't change the average that the formula is based on, but it does take more income out of the reach of Social Security's fund balance.

10. Broaden the tax base

This is one proposal that, if done correctly, is guaranteed to fix whatever ails Social Security. It will also fix the problems of high unemployment, low wages, and crumbling infrastructure. And it doesn't require specific steps designed to change Social Security. It does, however, require common sense steps to fix the major problems in the overall economy – reverse policies that create growing income inequality and create incentives for corporations and rich Americans to keep more wealth circulating in the economy instead of being moved overseas. Unfortunately, these steps are politically impossible unless we get a Congress that will quit demanding regressive policies.

Know the Facts before Spouting off About Welfare

(Originally published February 10, 2015 for The Blue Route Blog)

It's easy to complain about welfare if you don't understand what it is and what it does.

When you support cutting, gutting, or eliminating welfare because…

People on welfare are moochers who don't want to work.

Welfare is a drain on the economy and on society.

Welfare is fraught with fraud.

People on welfare can afford to buy things that you cannot afford.

You work hard for your money and you don't want to support society's "takers".

Too many people are on welfare.

Immigrants come here illegally in order to receive welfare benefits.

You don't believe in wealth or income redistribution.

Welfare is a symptom of a bloated federal government.

The government must live within its means, which means we can't afford welfare.

The government has no business handing out charity.

Welfare is unconstitutional.

Or any similar argument

Or even if you support drug testing as a means for eligibility

...perhaps you should put more thought into the implications of your position.

Such positions tend to treat the subject of welfare as an abstract. Quite frankly, it is easy to form opinions about an abstract concept such as welfare. The implications attached to simplistic statements about welfare as an abstract are far different from the implications attached to remarks made with knowledge of the details of welfare programs. If you care so much about your position on this issue that you take the time to share your opinion with others, then you should at least take a little time to learn the basic facts. At least get the facts straight so that you are not sharing your ignorance.

What is welfare?

Welfare consists of seven primary means-tested programs:

Temporary Assistance for Needy Families program (TANF)

Section 8 Housing Choice Voucher program

Supplemental Nutrition Program for Women, Infants, and Children (WIC)

Low Income Home Energy Assistance Program (LIHEAP)

Supplemental Nutrition Assistance Program (SNAP), also known as food stamps

Earned Income Tax Credit (EITC)

Medicaid

When you are talking about welfare in the United States, whether or not you are talking about cutting welfare, these are the specific programs you are talking about.

A description of each program starts here.

*

Temporary Assistance for Needy Families program (TANF)

For many people, TANF is what people mean when they talk about welfare; let's look at this program first.

TANF replaced AFDC as a result of welfare reform in the 1990s.

TANF programs are designed by each state. Each state decides which specific benefits are involved and the eligibility criteria, within certain guidelines from the federal government.

TANF is funded through block grants to states in exchange for setting up programs within the guidelines. States must also contribute to funding through "maintenance of effort" (MOE). States have the option of using MOE money for more generous benefits than benefits allowed through federal funds.

TANF programs must be designed to meet at least one of the following four criteria: 1. Provide assistance to needy families so that children can be cared for in their own homes 2. Reduce the dependency of needy parents by promoting job preparation, work and marriage 3. Prevent and reduce the incidence of out-of-wedlock pregnancies 4. Encourage the formation and maintenance of two-parent families.

Recipients must be adults who are responsible for raising children. Recipients must meet poverty guidelines. Recipients must be working towards employment or better employment. This may include studies toward a GED. Recipients who fail to meet guidelines are ineligible for benefits.

Benefits expire no later than 24 months after a recipient becomes eligible. There is a 60-month lifetime limit for benefits for any adult family member. States must stick to these limits for programs financed through federal block grants, but states are not forbidden from extending these limits for programs financed through their own MOE funds.

Immigrants are not eligible for this program unless they have been in the country legally for at least five years.

States have broad discretion in terms of denying benefits, but federal guidelines require that only families with children and pregnant women are eligible.

*

Section 8 Housing Choice Voucher program

The Section 8 Housing Choice Voucher program was created in the 1970s.

This program works through vouchers funded by the federal government, but the program is maintained by thousands of state and local housing agencies.

Congress decides on the formula used to distribute vouchers. 75% of new recipients each year must be at 30% of the poverty level or lower. Everybody else must be at 80% of the poverty level or lower.

The formula used by Congress gives preference to some specific types of families, such as families with homeless veterans.

Individuals and families can use their vouchers to obtain housing in the free market. Housing agencies verify that housing meets quality standards and is reasonably priced according to local market standards.

Individuals who use vouchers for rent assistance must pay at least 30% of their income on rent, or $50, whichever is higher.

Up to 20% of voucher funding goes towards subsidizing housing projects rather than going to eligible individuals.

Undocumented immigrants are not eligible.

*

Supplemental Nutrition Program for Women, Infants, and Children (WIC)

The WIC program was established in the 1970s. It is administered by individual states through USDA guidelines, and is funded through federal grants.

Specific benefits are designed for eligible women during each of the following time frames: during pregnancy, during post-pregnancy, during the breastfeeding stage, during the infants' first year following birth, and during a child's first 5 years.

Participants must meet categorical requirements.

Participants must meet residential requirements.

Participants must meet income requirements.

Participants must meet nutrition risk requirements.

Participants must receive medical check-ups and care.

The USDA determines which categories of items may be purchased with WIC checks, but states have leeway for determining eligible types and brands within each category.

WIC checks must be used at WIC-authorized businesses.

WIC checks must be used within a specified time frame.

Studies show that WIC reduces the incidence of low birth weight, reduces overall healthcare costs, and reduces federal spending.

*

Low Income Home Energy Assistance Program (LIHEAP)

LIHEAP was established in 1981 and is a part of the U.S. Department of Health and Human Services.

LIHEAP provides assistance for home heating bills to low-income households, with emphasis on households with disabled persons, elderly persons, and preschool-aged children.

This program is funded through federal block grants and other sources, but is administered entirely by various state agencies.

The formula for determining the amount of funding that goes to each agency is based on climate, economic, and demographic factors. Congress provides additional funding each year to be released during emergency situations, at the President's discretion.

The various state agencies set specific eligibility rules and determine how the funds get distributed to individual households, within broad federal guidelines.

LIHEAP is often operated on a first come, first served basis. When funds run out, state legislatures do have the option of providing additional funding.

*

Supplemental Nutrition Assistance Program (SNAP)

SNAP, commonly known as food stamps, is a program of the U.S. Department of Agriculture. Funding is authorized by Congress every five years as part of the Farm Bill.

SNAP is administered through various state agencies. Federal and state governments share in the administration costs of the program.

SNAP provides nutrition assistance to eligible low-income individuals and families.

SNAP benefits and eligibility rules have been changed numerous times – as part of welfare reform and whenever a new Farm Bill is authorized.

USDA specifically lists the following food items as being eligible: fruits and vegetables; breads and cereals; dairy products; meats, fish and poultry; and plants and seeds which are fit for household consumption.

USDA specifically lists the following items as ineligible: wine, beer, and liquor; cigarettes or tobacco; soaps; paper products; household supplies; pet foods; hot foods; food items that are consumable in the store; vitamins; and medicines.

In order to receive benefits, households must meet eligibility requirements regarding ownership of valuable assets.

Households must meet income requirements.

Maximum benefits for each household are based on the assumption that beneficiaries will spend 30% of their income on food items. The formula that is used to determine benefits includes a built-in work incentive.

Applicants must meet face-to-face with a caseworker and document that they meet income, expenses, and other eligibility requirements. State agencies are responsible for verifying all documented information.

Households with at least one able-bodied member of working age cannot receive SNAP benefits for more than three months in any 36-month period, unless the able-bodied household members are working or participating in a workfare employment and training program. They must accept any suitable employment that is offered to them.

Undocumented immigrants are not eligible for SNAP benefits. Also ineligible are workers out on strike, most college students, and legal immigrants with less than five years of residency, unless they have children in the household. Non-citizens in the country on temporary visas are not eligible.

75% of SNAP participants are in households with children. More than 25% are in households with elderly or disabled persons.

SNAP participation is highest during recessions and periods of high unemployment. SNAP is one of the most effective economic stimulus programs. Economic studies show that it generates $1.70 in economic activity for every dollar spent.

Grocery stores rely heavily on revenue from SNAP participants, and overwhelmingly oppose cuts in benefits.

Studies show that SNAP keeps millions of children out of poverty. Studies also show that SNAP reduces extreme poverty.

90% of SNAP benefits are spent on fruits & vegetables, grain products, meat, and dairy products.

According to the Government Accountability Office, the payment error rate is under 5%, with 2/3 of the errors being made by caseworkers and not by participants.

*

Earned Income Tax Credit (EITC)

The EITC is a once-a-year, means-tested tax credit that qualified low-income workers can claim on their income tax returns. Only people who work yet receive poverty wages qualify.

This credit is refundable, meaning that it can reduce a taxpayer's total income tax to below zero, providing a refund even if no taxes are owed. People who receive the EITC still must pay payroll taxes (Social Security, Medicare).

Many states have a similar credit on state income tax returns.

The EITC provides an incentive for low-income adults to work. The amount of the EITC increases when a qualified worker earns more money from working. Tax filers do not qualify for this credit unless they have income from working.

The EITC increases business activity and income for local businesses.

Fraudulent claims will result in taxpayers being barred from claiming this credit in future years.

The EITC began in 1975, but has been expanded several times since then. Historically, it has had broad bipartisan support. Even tax reforms designed to lower taxes, eliminate tax credits, or simplify tax returns (including the widely-publicized Tax Reform Act of 1986) have included an expansion of the EITC.

The EITC does little to help taxpayers who have no minor children. It is designed to help lift children out of poverty.

The EITC subsidizes the profits of companies by supplementing the incomes of workers who work for poverty wages, instead of requiring the employers to pay a living wage. When workers make a living wage, they do not qualify for EITC.

Studies show that the EITC is one of the most effective measures for moving children out of poverty. Studies also show that children fare better when they become adults if they have spent their childhood out of poverty.

Undocumented workers do not qualify for this tax credit.

*

Medicaid

Medicaid as we know it began in the 1980s when the federal government provided states with waivers to design managed-care programs.

Medicaid is a collection of many different programs, as determined at the state level.

Funding for Medicaid is shared among federal, state, and in some cases county levels of government.

Medicaid is means-tested, but low income is not the only eligibility requirement. States often make membership in certain categories a requirement – low-income children or low income senior citizens, for example.

Medicaid services and payment rates differ from state to state.

Some states provide lump-sum payments to private insurers for providing services to Medicaid patients (HIPP). Other states pay medical service providers directly on a fee-for-service basis.

Medicaid programs often pay for services which Medicare does not accept – dental care, for example.

***

Those are the seven major programs which collectively are "welfare". In addition to the above summaries of each, here are some general considerations to take into account:

These programs overwhelmingly are designed to help the most vulnerable among us: our children, elderly, and disabled citizens who live in poverty.

Many veterans rely on these programs.

These programs are means-tested, and as such are designed to not only help individuals escape poverty, but also to help the overall economy by reducing poverty rates.

These programs act as automatic stabilizers for the entire economy. Automatic stabilizers not only decrease the negative macroeconomic consequences of recessions and high unemployment, they also decrease long-term government debt.

We cannot balance the federal budget through gutting these programs. The math simply is not there. Many politicians who want to be known as deficit hawks like to target these programs, but doing so can only backfire. The reality is not the same as the rhetoric.

Everybody benefits when the overall poverty rate decreases.

Many businesses, especially local grocery stores, rely heavily on business from people in these programs. Business owners should understand that customers are not the enemy.

Other government policies – ones with a track record of reducing the effects of recessions, increasing employment, increasing wages, and renovating slum areas – are the most effective measures for reducing the need for welfare. Policies with a track record of benefitting corporations and very rich individuals at the expense of working-class people increase the need for welfare. Be sure you support the right kinds of policies if you truly desire a decrease in welfare.

Most of these programs are designed to help lift people out of poverty so that they don't need them in the future. Past welfare reform efforts have eliminated most of the true "welfare queens." Those on welfare today are not the same individuals as those on welfare in the past. Many people have gone through stages in life when they have fallen on hard times. Welfare helps to provide a safety net for these people, especially those who have no other safety net to fall back on. Millions of people every day are only one setback away from disaster, unless they have a safety net to fall back on.

People often make poor choices whenever they hit hard times. This is true for most of us, not just the ones who happen to be on today's welfare rolls. These same people make better choices when their situation doesn't seem so hopeless. Human decency (along with most religions) tells us to help people in need instead of watching them suffer while we blame them for their plight.

Making people on welfare pass drug tests – because we want to make them prove that they are "worthy" of our help – is ill-advised. Either we want to help people escape a desperate situation or we want to blame them for being desperate in the first place. Remember, these welfare programs are largely designed to help children. Making their parents "prove" to be worthy of our help will only harm the same children these programs are designed to help. We should not be condemning children because their parents might have made poor choices in a time of desperation.

These drug tests of welfare recipients have proven to cost many times more than the savings from denial of benefits. States which claim they must cut benefits for cost-effective programs in order to balance the budget are often the same states spending millions for a policy which is anything but cost-effective.

Children become more productive adults when they don't have to grow up in poverty.

Welfare has been reformed many times in the past, and can be reformed again in the future. Simply gutting these programs instead of fixing whatever specific problems exist in them is not a rational approach – this is a fix that doesn't target the problems. It makes no sense to gut entire programs because somebody somewhere might be receiving benefits improperly. Across-the-board cuts amount to throwing out the baby with the bath water.

Most of these programs rely on state agencies to verify that welfare money isn't spent fraudulently. Cutting welfare through reductions in the number of caseworkers, such as many states have done, only serves to increase the chances for fraud.

Undocumented immigrants do not qualify for these programs. Legal immigrants must wait up to five years to qualify for many of these programs.

Studies show that fraud rates are low for most of these programs. Studies also show that these programs are effective in doing what they are designed to do. That doesn't mean they cannot be improved.

The fact that studies show that these programs are effective means that they are consistent with the goals set forth in the preamble to the Constitution. They are not charity for some; they benefit all.

Much of this analysis also applies to unemployment insurance, but I haven't included unemployment because unemployment compensation is not welfare. It is an entitlement.

Fact: at today's federal minimum wage, a two-parent family with two children and one full-time minimum wage worker lives below the poverty line, unless they receive benefits from some of these welfare programs.

If you know all of this, and you still want to argue for cutting or eliminating welfare, you are free to do so. In order for your arguments to be rational rather than reactionary, they should include knowledge of how these specific programs affect various groups of people, and the overall economy itself. A generic and abstract reference to "welfare" doesn't qualify as a rational argument.

Section 12: Rational and Practical vs. Irrational and Theoretical

"An Age of Enlightenment for 21st Century America"

"Use Facts to Counter Political Arguments which are based on Theories and Misconceptions"

"Identifying Fallacies of Logic in Today's Political Arguments"

"List of Logical Fallacies Commonly Used in Political Arguments"

An Age of Enlightenment for 21st Century America

(Originally published March 30, 2015 for The Blue Route Blog)

The men who collaborated to create the United States Constitution were far from unanimous in their beliefs.

The delegates to the Constitutional Convention in 1787 were a diverse group of individuals. The dominant power brokers of the day – New England merchants and Virginia plantation owners – were represented. The interests of small states and large states were both represented. These men had diverse religious beliefs, and diverse beliefs on how power should be shared among various levels of government.

Today, we contribute to the dumbing-down of America when we cherry-pick statements from some of these founders in order to project their words into today's political, economic, social, and technological realities. These men were a diverse group, but they had two very important things in common:

1. They were thinkers. Nearly all of them were men of the Enlightenment.

2. They took a practical approach to government. They were interested in creating something that would work in the real world. They were less interested in conforming to a particular political philosophy.

We, on the other hand, live in an age in which – much too often – ignorance is considered to be a political virtue. People today are scoring political points by rewriting history to fit a political agenda; by denying scientific evidence; by downplaying the contributions of education and educators; and by ignoring practical economics in favor of disproven economic theories. People are ignoring real evidence that doesn't fit their political agenda, while accepting misinformation and outright untruths without question or evidence. At the same time, the words of the founders and the Constitution itself are often cherry-picked and twisted as justification for a political agenda.

This is NOT the approach that the founders took. We desperately need a new Age of Enlightenment in 21st century America. We need leaders who respect knowledge instead of mocking it. We need leaders who accept scientific evidence instead of mocking it. We need leaders who learn from history instead of re-writing it to fit an agenda. We need leaders who have a higher regard for education itself.

Before we get the leaders we need, we have to elect them. We have to be practical about doing this, however. We can't stop willfully-ignorant citizens from voting, but perhaps we can do a much better job of organizing a counterattack against ignorance and misinformation. We already have advocates for scientific evidence. We have advocates for historical accuracy. We have advocates for education. We have advocates for reality-based politics and economics. In my mind, these advocates should unite, but alter their messages.

Currently, the messages from these advocates tend to take the form of "we are right, and you are wrong," or perhaps "my political party is better than your political party." Regardless of the amount of truth in such statements, this is precisely the method used by opponents. As a result, advocates on each side end up "preaching to the choir." People on both sides dig in, and few minds are changed. I would suggest that an important step is missing from these types of arguments. Before the discussion turns to specific issues and party differences, advocates for truth and knowledge should focus on truth and knowledge as their primary talking points. Create a large bloc of individuals whose main uniting principle is truth and knowledge. If this could be accomplished, the talking points on specific issues would follow along.

Without this step, we will continue to preach to the choir and suffer from ignorance and division. With this step – assuming advocates are united enough and vocal enough – perhaps fewer people would consider ignorance to be a virtue.

In short, we need a new Age of Enlightenment to take hold. We can start by understanding the unifying principles of our founding fathers.

Men of the Enlightenment

The founding fathers were not united by a belief in a specific structure of government. They were not united by a common religious belief. Here is what the founders WERE united on, by general consensus:

The founding fathers believed that knowledge was a virtue, and ignorance was not. They welcomed scientific knowledge and would never think of mocking science in order to make political statements. They would never mock educated people as being somehow inferior to the uneducated. The founders were some of the most educated of Americans, but they did not believe that education belonged to an elite few. They did not wish to control the masses through ignorance, but instead they believed that widespread knowledge and education were vital to the survival of our system of representative government.

The founders built upon the knowledge of others, and did not hesitate to study whatever sources were available. They studied philosophers such as Voltaire and Rousseau; they studied the ancient Greeks and Romans; they learned about governments in other countries; they studied the Magna Carta and the entire known world history of governing constitutions (including our own state constitutions); they studied theology and theocracies; they studied religious documents, including the Bible.

The founders were united in opposition to state-sponsored religion. This did not prevent them from gaining knowledge through the study of religious documents. They were interested in knowledge from all available sources. Opposition to state-sponsored religion did not prevent them from exercising their personal beliefs. They simply did not use concepts such as "because God said so in the Bible" in order to rationalize their ideas for government.

The founders were united in favor of representative government, with politicians answerable to the people. As part of this, they were united in favor of a free press which held government officials accountable.

The founders were united in mistrust of powerful corporations and political parties.

Those who signed the Constitution, and those who voted to ratify it, knew that they were creating a stronger central government; doing so was the only reason for the Constitutional Convention in the first place.

Practicality

Above all, the founders took a practical approach to government. They were interested in what worked and why. They learned from the great philosophers, but they did so from a distance and considered the practicality of what the philosophers had to say. They studied what had worked and hadn't worked in the history of government. They built on the knowledge of others, but they had a lot to say about what they had learned through their own experiences of being British subjects, of fighting a war of independence and of running the governments of newly-free states.

As a result of this practical experience...

The founders insisted that people subject to laws be represented in the legislative process.

They did not trust political parties.

They did not trust powerful corporations.

They opposed a standing army in American towns and streets.

They knew that ratification would be extremely problematic, and they compromised whenever necessary. Rather than ending up with a Constitution that coincided with anybody's wishes, the "final product" was filled with numerous compromises, based on the delegates' practical experience and the prospects for ratification. A couple of these compromises stand out as being particularly noteworthy: The Great Compromise, which settled the biggest stumbling block of the convention by creating a bicameral legislature in which the states would have equal representation in the Senate but proportional representation in the House of Representatives; and the 3/5 Rule, which allowed the process to proceed without permanently settling the issue of slavery. Without these compromises, there would have been no possibility of ratification. The Union likely would have failed under the Articles of Confederation, and there never would have been a United States Constitution to serve as a blueprint for future constitutions around the world. The United States as we know it would not exist.

The founding fathers were far from perfect human beings. Individually, they often failed to live up to their own ideals (for example, while in office they sometimes resorted to degrading political rhetoric instead of rational debate); some of them lived a life that would be considered morally reprehensible by today's standards (for example, owning slaves). Collectively, they failed to foresee some political developments which they most certainly would not approve of (for example the rise of dominant political parties and powerful corporations). They could not settle the issue of slavery. They would not consider allowing women to participate in the political process, including the right to vote.

In spite of these shortcomings, they gave themselves a chance to succeed – within the political realities of their day – because they used an approach based on an appreciation of knowledge and practical governing. They did not sneer at knowledge in order to appeal to mankind's baser instincts; they welcomed their position as men of the Enlightenment.

We live in an era of different political realities. We have the advantage of being able to learn from the experiences of our founding fathers. Yet our hands are tied by political polarization which we have created ourselves. We mock education, scientific knowledge, historical facts, and economic reality instead of welcoming them. We have given ourselves no chance to succeed in the ways our founders succeeded.

In order to move forward, we desperately need to usher in a new Age of Enlightenment.

Use Facts to Counter Political Arguments which are based on Theories and Misconceptions

(Originally published September 15, 2014 for The Blue Route Blog)

"An Ounce of Action is Worth a Ton of Theory" ~ Ralph Waldo Emerson

*

I groan every time I hear somebody invoke the Econ 101 argument. That's the argument over policy that goes like this:

"My position is right because they teach it in econ 101, and if you don't agree with me then you don't understand basic economics".

This type of argument seems to be most prevalent among conservatives:

"If we raise the minimum wage, then minimum wage workers will lose their jobs. There will be fewer jobs in the economy. If you knew basic economics, you would agree with me."

"If we raise the minimum wage, then nobody will gain because all of the cost increase will be passed on to consumers in the form of higher prices. If you knew basic economics, you would agree with me."

"The reason unemployment is high is because taxes on the rich and on corporations are too high. If you understood basic economics, you would know that higher taxes decrease production and jobs."

"The Federal Reserve's policies are creating high inflation. Too much money chasing too few goods results in nothing but high inflation. Anybody who stayed awake in Econ 101 knows this."

"The economy would be more stable if we returned to the gold standard. Basic economics says that nothing will hold its value if we use worthless pieces of paper as a currency."

…and on and on.

These types of arguments appeal to theory, yet they show a lack of understanding of the theories that they appeal to. For the record, Econ 101 does NOT state as a fact that if a specific policy is adopted in the real world, then a specific outcome will follow. For example, basic economics does not say that if you raise the minimum wage, then the economy will lose jobs. Whoever makes such a claim is the one who must have fallen asleep during an Econ 101 lecture. You see, economics models and theories are not designed to tell you as a fact that a specific outcome will follow a specific policy. Economics models and theories always involve more than a simple "if A, then B" logical argument. Far too often, people of all levels of learning in the field of economics make this simple mistake. All they take away from what they have learned is that "if A, then B". Yet the source they are citing never actually says "if A, then B". Instead, the models and theories always involve more. There are numerous assumptions necessary to make these models and theories work logically – assumptions such as ceteris paribus (all else held equal or constant), a starting and ending point of a general equilibrium, and all of the assumptions of simpler models that the one in question is based on, just to name a few of many. The point is that all of these assumptions are required in order to make any conclusions valid, and all of these assumptions are not typically met in the real world. Logically, each of the assumptions adds another "if" to the if-then equation. Instead of "if A, then B", all economic models and theories use the equation "if A, and if C, and if D, and…if N, then B". Drawing a conclusion in the real world that "if A, then B" is not rational.

But rational, or not, there is a much more effective and accurate way to make a case in a debate over policy, which is the main point of this essay. Good heavens, why would anybody need to mention what some theory says will happen, when we have an extensive historical record that will tell us exactly what has happened? Why say that jobs will be lost if the minimum wage goes up when we have a long record that says otherwise?

I have seen this numerous times on social media: Somebody makes a claim by appealing to what is supposedly said in Econ 101, and then somebody making the opposite claim simply concedes the point. Both end up believing something that isn't true. Please, take a look at the big-picture historical record before conceding any point that you are trying to make. Don't accept theory as a valid point unless you know that the historical record actually backs it up. Refer to the quote above by Emerson. Take action, and look up the record. Such action will be worth more than an appeal to theory.

The historical record is extensive. It isn't valid to suggest that the historical record is wrong due to other factors affecting the economy. If there is no pattern in such an extensive record to support a claim based on theory, then the theory is not a valid argument for the claim.

Identifying Fallacies of Logic in Today's Political Arguments

(Originally published August 18, 2014 for The Blue Route Blog)

Have you ever discussed partisan issues with somebody, and you just knew that their arguments were somehow invalid, but you couldn't pinpoint exactly how to point this out and respond accordingly? Do you want to make sure that you are only using valid arguments yourself so that you don't get caught being the irrational one in an argument?

What about politicians and political talking heads? Other than when they straight-out lie to you, how can you tell when they are saying things that are rational as opposed to playing on emotions by saying things that sound reasonable according to your baser instincts?

Here is a list of logical fallacies that can help. Keep these fallacies in mind, or keep this list handy, when debating issues with someone who disagrees with you. You can become the rational one in debates.

Keep this list in mind while listening to political arguments from politicians and talking heads.

Fallacies of logic are, quite simply, errors in reasoning. They are irrational arguments. They can be distinguished from factual errors, which are fallacies but not logical fallacies. Logical fallacies have been studied and categorized for centuries, dating back to the days of Plato and Aristotle. Many are known by names that are in the Latin language, which is evidence of the antiquity of their study.

Although known types of fallacies have become quite standardized over time, it is difficult to find one list of fallacies that is

208

comprehensive. Many are very similar, with differences that are irrelevant in most situations. Many are specific cases of other, more general fallacies. Some can be classified in subsets with different combinations of others.

This list is not comprehensive, but it is rather extensive. I have made no attempt to put them in any form of hierarchy. Some have come to be known by more than one name, and I have grouped together some with only nuanced differences. These differences are irrelevant for the purpose at hand. Since different names are used together, this list is not in alphabetical order. I have chosen to list only the types of fallacies which are common today in political debates.

You will likely find that this list reads like an academic study. No doubt, you have already heard of some of these. But unless you have studied logic in a formal educational setting, you probably won't want to jump right in, reading the list and studying it until you have this information down pat. You probably want to get to the arguments first, and then see how to counter those arguments with logic.

With that in mind, here are several samples of common arguments used in today's political environment. You might have seen these recently. Perhaps you have seen many of them on several occasions. All of them are invalid because they rely on logical fallacies.

The ones within quotation marks use typical wording of arguments; the ones without quotation marks describe the arguments. Each example includes an explanation of the fallacies involved. The names of the relevant fallacies are given in bold. You can then go to the list of fallacies which follows, and find a definition and more information for each fallacy. Familiarity with this process will help you to identify and counter fallacies of logic in arguments other than the samples that I use here.

***

"Capitalism is all about the private sector. It works because of the 'invisible hand'. Therefore, any government involvement is socialism."

This argument incorporates a number of different fallacies of logic. It mischaracterizes the role and nature of the government, in both capitalism and socialism, by ignoring facts such as:

The government creates the circumstances that make a system of capitalism possible; no system of pure capitalism - one with no government involvement - has ever existed or ever could exist; and socialism by definition requires government ownership of some factors of production. The fact that the government plays some kind of role in the economy, short of ownership of the factors of production, is not an indication of socialism. By using a false definition of socialism, and implying a false role for government in capitalism, a generic argument against government involvement is a straw man argument. Every economy necessarily includes a role for government as well as a role for market forces. Ignoring the reality of various types of mixed economies and substituting arguments for capitalism over socialism is oversimplification and creates a false dilemma. The wording of the argument by itself doesn't necessarily claim a support for capitalism over socialism, but it doesn't have to. This common argument is associated with implicit ad nauseam comments that make it clear that the arguer considers capitalism to be unquestionably good and socialism to be so evil as to be avoided. **(False dilemma; Playing on emotions; Oversimplifying; Argumentum ad nauseam; Straw man; Judgmental language)**

*

"Rich people pay the majority of taxes, and poor people receive handouts from the government which are paid for with rich people's taxes. Therefore, this problem is caused by the rich people's taxes being too high."

This is only one example of a number of different arguments relating to inequality. It ignores the fact that inequality has grown at the same time that effective tax rates on the rich have decreased significantly. Both the increase in inequality and the decrease in tax rates for the rich have been historically large in recent decades. This means that, mathematically, the consequences of rich people paying a higher share of the taxes while more government handouts are going to poor people can only be caused by rich people receiving a higher share of taxable income while the poor receive a smaller share of taxable income. In fact, this is verified by the historical record. But this argument is making the opposite claim, saying that the problem is due to tax rates on rich people being too high. In effect, this argument advocates for more of the types of policies which created the inequality, while leaving the impression that rich people's tax rates have increased - which is false. However, many people have heard the claim so often that they assume it to be true. **(Circular cause and consequence; Argumentum ad nauseam; Lying with statistics)**

*

"Corporate executives earn all of the money that they are paid, because they are paid according to the free market."

This argument is used to justify corporate executives receiving a much larger share of national income than they did in the past, while the workers they employ receive a much smaller share. It ignores the fact that no market forces can be identified to explain it. There is no market for corporate executives which works according to the principles of classic economics behind such claims; the pay scale is not based on relative productivity or efficiency; and the market does not act in accordance with the theories of perfect competition that are implied in the claim. Claiming that it is earned according to the market is the same thing as: "Corporate executives earn all of the money that they are paid." "How do you know that they earn it?" "Because that is what they get paid." **(Circular Argument; non sequitur)**

*

Stating the dangers of a completely disarmed population when the opposition is not arguing for disarming the population, but rather arguing for a few gun control laws designed to improve safety.

I can't think of any issue that is more emotionally-charged than the issue of gun control. For many people, this is a partisan issue. For others, it is a highly personal issue unrelated to other political issues. The nature of the issue means that many different kinds of arguments involving logical fallacies are involved. Here, I'm only focusing on a current trend, whereby many arguments against any kind of gun law are factually just arguments against a total gun ban, which is not the argument that the opposition is making. **(Straw Man)**

*

"Trickle-down economics works because the economy grew and government revenue increased after Reagan lowered taxes."

This statement cherry-picks "economy grew", "government revenue increased" and "lowered taxes" from the following evidence, the totality of which would lead to a different conclusion:

Ronald Reagan took office in January of 1981. The economy went into a recession in July of 1981 and stayed in recession until November of 1982. This followed a shorter recession from January

1980 to July 1980. The annual unemployment rate peaked at 9.7% in 1982, which is still the highest on record. The economy grew following the recession, as it always does following a recession. It continued to grow until a new recession began in July 1990. The economic growth following the recession of 1981-1982 was accomplished using the classical Keynesian policies of massive government debt and large increases in government spending, the opposite of what this argument implies. Several changes occurred in the tax code throughout these years, most notably the Tax Reform Act of 1986. Some taxes decreased, some increased; some loopholes were closed. Government deficits and debt grew far out of proportion to anything seen before, due to a much larger increase in government expenditures over revenue. In dollar terms, revenue for the most part increased due to an increase in the size of the economy as well as population growth. In terms of percentage of the economy and percentage of expenditures, revenue decreased. What was non-Keynesian about this method of escape from recession is the long term nature of fixes for a short term problem. Deficits continued to skyrocket even after the goal of economic growth was reached; a "no new tax" and deregulatory mentality developed that negatively affected future decades. Without going into detail here, it can be argued using historical data that the long term problems far outpaced the short term economic gains. The conclusion that "trickle-down economics works" agrees with the cherry-picked aspects but not with the totality of the scenario. **(Stacked Evidence; Reductionism)**

*

"The Republican Party is the party of Lincoln."

This argument is used to imply that the modern Republican Party shares the values of Abraham Lincoln, or that Lincoln would approve of the modern-day party positions. Similar arguments are made regarding the Republican Party and the Civil Rights movement in the 1960s. The argument ignores the fact that the make-up and direction of the party has shifted and evolved into something completely different from what it used to be. For details, see the historical record of party registration changes from Southern Democrats opposed to civil rights, and the Republican Party's Southern Strategy. **(Etymological fallacy; Presentism)**

*

Only referencing or linking a source from a blog or other post from somebody who is paid to agree with a particular position as a basis for an argument, while ignoring any contrary information that comes from qualified sources. **(False attribution)**

*

Journalists often assume that they are being unbiased if they give equal time to each side of an issue, and report each position as equal, regardless of the relative merits of each position. **(False compromise)**

*

The idea that the meaning of the Constitution cannot be changed, and must be strictly adhered to and applied to modern situations, regardless of any subsequent human advancements or changes in global conditions. **(Historian's fallacy)**

*

"Households and businesses must live within their budgets, so the government should never run a deficit."

This argument implicitly defines a deficit as "paying bills on time" for households and businesses, while at the same time it defines a deficit as "not having any bills to pay" for the government; two different definitions that together make the case. In reality, most households, businesses, and governments routinely use credit, and all presumably are expected to pay their bills on time. The U.S. government actually has a much better record in terms of "paying

214

bills on time" than households or businesses. In fact, the U.S. government is considered the safest investment in the world, and the U.S. dollar is a global currency due to the government's stellar credit record. **(Inconsistent comparison)**

*

"I oppose welfare because I don't want my hard-earned money going to lazy people who choose to live off handouts. I don't want money from 'makers' going to 'takers'." Or, finding a specific example of apparent welfare fraud and using it to argue that welfare should be abolished or greatly curtailed.

Welfare fraud is already illegal, and the laws making it illegal can always be reviewed and tightened if necessary. Citizens who have factual knowledge that welfare fraud is taking place can report this to the state authorities in charge instead of making sweeping generalizations that imply widespread fraud. This is not a valid argument for eliminating or greatly curtailing the welfare system outside of the specific fraud aspect, but it does play on people's emotions by getting them to think that their tax money is going to benefit somebody who is not worthy. **(Sweeping generalization; Overwhelming exception; Playing on emotions; Argumentum ad nauseam)**

*

"I oppose legalizing gay marriage because…"

I left this one as a fill-in-the-blank sentence because what is in the rest of the sentence most likely does not matter. I have followed the issue extensively and I have seen many arguments on both sides. All of the arguments that I have seen in opposition to legalizing gay marriage are examples of one or more of the following fallacies of logic: **(Non sequitur; Blind loyalty; Argumentum ad numerum; Slippery slope; Argumentum ad**

215

antiquitatem; Appeal to nature; Contextomy; Nunc pro tunc;
Wishful thinking; Judgmental language; Reductionism)

*

"Taxing corporations kills jobs."

"Minimum wage jobs are only temporary jobs for teenagers or
entry-level positions."

"More and more regulations are hurting business."

"Obama is raising our taxes to pay for out of control
government spending."

"Obama is bankrupting America with record high deficits."

"Obama has ignored the Constitution and is acting like a
dictator with all of his executive orders."

"All inflation is caused by an increase in the money supply."

These are examples of beliefs that are commonly held, yet all of
them can either be proven false, or the available evidence does not
support the arguments. **(Argumentum ad nauseam)**

List of Logical Fallacies Commonly Used in Political Arguments

The list of logical fallacies begins on the next page. Keep in mind that this list is not comprehensive, but has been compiled in an attempt to include the fallacies which are common in today's political arguments. Since many fallacies are known by different names, differences between others are only subtle differences which are irrelevant to the purpose here, and many fallacies can be considered both stand-alone fallacies and sub-categories of other fallacies, this list is not in any particular order. I have grouped identical and nearly identical ones together.

Petitio principia (Begging the question)

Circulus in demonstrando (Circular argument)

Assuming the conclusion

This is the fallacy of using what you are trying to prove as part of the proof. The conclusion is merely a restatement of the premise.

*

*

Argumentum ad nauseam

Argument from Repetition

Big lie technique

Staying on message

This is the fallacy of trying to prove something simply by making the same claim so often that the listener assumes that if it is said so often it must be true. Whether or not the claim itself is fallacious is irrelevant; it is only by repetition of the claim that this fallacy is committed. Whether or not a claim is true, stating it over and over again doesn't make it so.

.*

*

Cum hoc ergo propter hoc (With this, therefore because of this)

Post hoc ergo propter hoc (After this, therefore because of this)

False cause

This is the fallacy of concluding causation based on correlation. Just because two events happen together doesn't necessarily mean that one caused the other.

Non sequitur

"It does not follow"

The conclusion is not drawn logically from the evidence presented.

*

*

Straw man

This is the fallacy of mischaracterizing the position of an opponent and arguing against that mischaracterization rather than the actual position of the opponent.

*

*

Stacked evidence

Confirmation bias

Half truths

Observational selection

Lying with statistics

These types of fallacies involve cherry-picking pieces of evidence so that a distorted conclusion is drawn.

Either-or

Taboo

There is no alternative

Get over it

Fait accompli

These types of fallacies involve presenting a black and white worldview in which only one or two choices are considered as if no other option is possible; they could involve an attempt to end debate by taking options off the table.

*

*

Red herring

The red herring fallacy involves the use of arguments that are irrelevant to the question at hand; or the use of any diversionary tactics that are designed to change the subject in order to get the person you are debating to talk about something other than the issue at hand.

Dicto simpliciter

Sweeping generalization

Hasty generalization

Anecdotal

Texas sharpshooter

These are variations on the same type of fallacy, a fallacy of stereotyping: presenting specific examples in arguments and then drawing conclusions as if the evidence is true in every case.

Argumentum ad hominem

Poisoning the well

Personal attack

This fallacy occurs when an arguer makes attacks on the person instead of the person's ideas that are at issue.

*

*

Tu quoque

You too

Appeal to hypocrisy

Two wrongs make a right

This is a type of red herring in which the arguer, when presented with evidence of committing a logical fallacy, instead of admitting to error, responds with the claim that the opponent also has committed the same (or worse) fallacy.

Guilt by Association

This is the fallacy of attacking an opponent's associates instead of the ideas presented.

Argumentum ad verecundiam

Appeal to authority

Blind loyalty

Blind obedience

Nuremberg defense

Blood is thicker than water

Testimonial

These are variations of the same type of fallacy. They involve citing the beliefs or words of somebody who is considered to have a good character or reputation as evidence, even though that person is not an authority on the issue at hand; or taking a position simply to agree with somebody for personal reasons.

*

*

Argumentum ad numerum (Appeal to numbers)

Argumentum ad populum (Appeal to the public)

Bandwagon appeal

Argument from common sense

These fallacies involve using evidence of the popularity of a belief to argue that the belief is right or true.

Slippery slope

Camel's nose

This fallacy involves arguing that if one thing is allowed to happen, it will lead to other things with negative consequences, but without providing evidence that logically links the issue at hand with the consequences. Because the fallacy is the missing evidence supporting the claim, this is a form of non sequitur.

*

*

Argumentum ad antiquitatem

Appeal to antiquity or tradition

This is the argument that a certain way of doing something is the correct way simply because that is the way it has traditionally been done.

*

*

Argumentum ad ignorantiam (Argument from ignorance)

Argumentum e silentio (Argument from silence)

These are similar fallacies that involve assuming something is true simply because it has not been proven false, or cannot be proven false (argumentum ad ignorantiam); arguing that something is false because it hasn't been proven true (argumentum e silentio).

Argumentum ad logicam

Argument to logic

Fallacy fallacy

This fallacy involves claiming something is false simply because someone has offered an invalid argument for it.

*

*

Argumentum ad misericordiam

Appeal to pity

This is the argument that "something must be done and you need to do more", without recognizing that other worthwhile causes exist, different people place different priorities on these causes, resources are limited, and "doing something" does not necessarily create effective and efficient results.

*

*

Plurium interrogationum

Complex question

Loaded question

Fallacy of many questions

Have you stopped beating your wife?

This is a question that is worded in such a way as to imply that something is true even if that truth has not been established, often in a form requiring a yes or no answer.

Appeal to nature

Appeal to God's will

Appeal to faith

These types of fallacies are arguments that assume that whatever the arguer considers consistent with nature or the arguer's belief in a higher power is good, and whatever conflicts with this definition of nature is bad.

*

*

Naturalistic fallacy

Is-ought fallacy

This is the fallacy of reaching conclusions of good or bad based on facts alone. Conclusions of value must include premises of value in order to be valid.

*

*

Circular cause and consequence

This fallacy involves the claim that the consequence of something is what caused it.

*

*

Equivocation

The fallacy of equivocation occurs from making a misleading statement by using a term that has more than one definition, and implying that one definition is being used when in fact the context requires a different definition.

Ecological fallacy

This fallacy involves making assumptions about specific individuals based solely on conclusions drawn from a larger group that these individuals are perceived to be a part of.

*

*

Etymological fallacy

This fallacy involves the inference that the current meaning of a term is the same as its original or historical meaning.

*

*

False dilemma

False dichotomy

Black and white fallacy

Excluded middle

Two opposing positions are assumed to be the only possibilities.

*

*

If-by-whiskey

Doublespeak

Ambiguity

This fallacy involves using carefully selected words which can be implied to support whichever side of an issue the listener supports.

False attribution

False attribution involves the use of biased, irrelevant, unqualified, falsified, or unidentified sources to support arguments.

Contextomy

Fallacy of quoting out of context

This fallacy involves using selected words from a source with the result of distorting the contextual meaning of the source.

*

*

Argument to moderation

False compromise

Middle ground

This fallacy occurs by assuming or implying that the truth or best outcome lies somewhere between two opposing viewpoints.

*

*

Nunc pro tunc

Presentism

This is the practice of rewriting history by projecting present day positions and issues into the past in a way that implies historical agreement with those positions.

*

*

Historian's fallacy

This fallacy involves an implicit assumption that the information we have available today was also available to decision-makers of the past.

Inconsistent comparison

This fallacy involves comparing or contrasting two ideas but using different methods for each idea.

*

*

Ignoratio elenchi

Irrelevant conclusion

Missing the point

This is an argument that does not actually address the issue at hand.

*

*

Kettle logic

This is the practice of continuing to defend a position against evidence to the contrary by using multiple arguments that are not consistent with each other.

*

*

Moving the goalposts

Raising the bar

Special pleading

These are similar types of fallacies that involve demanding more and stronger evidence from an opponent, or creating exceptions, when confronted with evidence that contradicts one's position.

Nirvana fallacy

Perfect solution fallacy

This is the fallacy of rejecting a proposed solution to a problem because it is not perfect, even if no perfect solution has been proposed.

*

*

Onus probandi incumbit ei qui dicit, non ei qui negat

Burden of proof

Denying a negative

This fallacy involves making a claim and then demanding that someone disprove the claim. It is a specific form of argumentum ad ignorantiam.

Argumentum verbosium

Proof by verbosity

Proof by intimidation

Shotgun argumentation

Snow job

This is the fallacy of making a claim that is so complex or wordy that no opponent can possibly deal with all of the different components of the claim, especially when a time limit is involved.

Misleading vividness

Overwhelming exception

These are similar types of fallacies that involve using a detailed description of an event (misleading vividness) or citing a notorious example (overwhelming exception) to imply that the problem is much bigger than that one event, and concluding that a bigger problem needs to be addressed.

*

*

Wishful thinking

This is the practice of basing arguments on what a debater wants to be true, rather than on what the evidence says is true.

Appeal to motive

This is the fallacy of rejecting an argument because of perceived motives of the person making the argument, instead of addressing the merits of the argument.

*

*

Bulverism

Psychogenetic Fallacy

This is the fallacy of rejecting an idea solely because the person proposing the idea is thought or known to be biased. It is a form of argumentum ad hominem in the sense that it is only a fallacy if it involves the bias of the person rather than the bias of an idea.

Judgmental language fallacy

This is the practice of using insults or words with negative connotations in order to influence the listener.

*

*

Reductio ad hitlerum

Playing the Nazi card

This fallacy involves attempting to associate opponents with somebody who is universally reviled. It is a specific form of judgmental language fallacy.

Personal incredulity

This involves rejecting an argument because it is too difficult to understand.

*

*

Argument from consequences

Argument from inertia

Stay the course

These types of fallacies occur when an arguer refuses to admit an error in reasoning, perhaps by citing dire consequences of the opposing position.

Reductionism

Oversimplifying

Sloganeering

Playing on emotions

Sob story

These are similar fallacies of arguments using simplistic statements or emotionally charged language to mislead by making a complex situation sound simple.

About the Author

Jerry Wyant

Author of the following books:

Basic Economics for Students and Non-Students Alike

Sanity and Public Policy: Separating Truth from Truisms

Making Education Work

Even Great Doctors Make Mistakes

Common Misconceptions of Economic Policy

Creator of the website www.economicsonlinetutor.com

Creator and administrator of the following Facebook pages:

Economics Online Tutor

Making Education Work

You can follow Jerry on Twitter @jawyant

www.ingramcontent.com/pod-product-compliance
Lightning Source LLC
Chambersburg PA
CBHW051901170526
45168CB00001B/196

* 9 7 8 1 5 1 7 4 8 4 9 7 2 *